THE HOME UNIVERSITY LIBRARY
OF MODERN KNOWLEDGE

218

SEVENTEENTH-CENTURY
ENGLISH LITERATURE

Seventeenth-Century English Literature

C. V. WEDGWOOD

LONDON
OXFORD UNIVERSITY PRESS
NEW YORK   TORONTO

Oxford University Press, Amen House, London E.C.4

GLASGOW NEW YORK TORONTO MELBOURNE WELLINGTON
BOMBAY CALCUTTA MADRAS KARACHI LAHORE DACCA
CAPE TOWN SALISBURY NAIROBI IBADAN ACCRA
KUALA LUMPUR HONG KONG

First published 1950
Reprinted in 1956 *and* 1963

Printed in Great Britain by
Butler and Tanner Ltd, Frome and London

CONTENTS

59759

Contents

v

CHAPTER I

INTRODUCTORY

A SHORT general history of English literature in the seventeenth century can give no more than approximate directions for crossing a complicated, various, and sometimes clouded landscape. Before certain famous views every guide must halt: that mountain peak is Milton, this delightful grove is Dryden. But the selection and rejection of lesser beauties must depend on the caprice of the writer.

There is probably more to be gained than lost from regarding the seventeenth century simply as a division of a hundred years: 1600 to 1700. The political historian, when he speaks of this century, may mean 1603 to 1714 if he makes it coincide roughly with the Stuart dynasty; or 1603 to 1689 if he makes it coincide with the constitutional struggle for Parliamentary control over the Crown. It is sometimes divided again at 1642, when the Civil War broke out, or, more usually, at 1660, when King Charles II was restored. None of these dates is helpful in literary history. At least the round dates which begin and end the century make no claim to be more than ciphers. Since all the divisions which the writer or the teacher must insert for the sake of convenience in the continuous process of human evolution are more or less arbitrary, there is something to be said for selecting those which are evidently so, in preference to those which have a deceptive appearance of reason.

This book, therefore, is chiefly concerned with the literature of the English language written in the hundred years between 1600 and 1700, although there may be a little backward glancing here and a little overrunning there to explain the origins of such a thing or to point the future of such another.[1]

The seventeenth century was a time of exuberant activity, of experiment in politics, speculation in religion, investigation in the natural sciences, and argument everywhere. The heavens came under the scrutiny of the telescope which soon revealed the mystery of the Milky Way to be nothing more extraordinary than the 'confused light of small stars, like so many nails in a door'. As for the great globe itself, the scientists could not let it alone. 'The world', wrote Robert Burton, 'is tossed in a blanket amongst them; they hoyse the earth up and down like a ball, make it stand or give at their pleasure.'

Doctors disputed over the body of man, anatomists dissected and demonstrated on the corpses supplied for a consideration by the public executioner, and physiologists inserted fragments of their tissue under the recently invented microscope. Inventors displayed for public attention, with or without success, knitting frames and pressure-cookers, unupsettable coaches, paddle-boats, more powerful explosives and more reliable watches, more ingenious fountains and more spectacular fire-

---

[1] Shakespeare, who belongs in time both to the sixteenth and the seventeenth centuries, has been left to the author of a projected volume on *Sixteenth-Century English Literature* in this series.

works, telescopes and surgical instruments, portable cannon and case-shot.

Travellers, zealously investigating the paths already opened by a century of exploration, thrust their way into the heart of Persia or up the huge rivers of the American continent, reached the courts of the Great Mogul and of the Tsar of Muscovy. Traders, following immediately behind them, brought back to the shops of Covent Garden and the Exchange furs and amber and parakeets, ostrich plumes and silk and cotton, spice and currants and pineapples, coffee and tea and chocolate. An elephant—from Africa or from India?—was to be seen in London. In Scotland 'His Majesty's Camel' was licensed to be led from place to place and shown to the people by tuck of drum, except during sermon-time on the Sabbath.

In politics the time was pregnant of a hundred theories, some monstrous births but more that were sane and valuable: in Scotland the narrow theocracy of the Presbyterians flourished briefly in an unblessed collaboration with a decaying feudal power; in Ireland benevolent and less benevolent despotisms alternated with anarchy; in England the royal authority struggled, underhand or in the open, with the Parliamentarianism of an ambitious landed class, and the egalitarian doctrines of the Levellers flamed suddenly and were suddenly extinguished. In religion, moods ranging from a rancorous zeal to an amiable pietism gave birth to a multitude of sects, some fertile in literature, most in propaganda, all in preachers.

In this talk, in this speculation, in the quarrels and the compromises, the English language developed to a rich maturity. All through the century it was growing on the tongues of the ordinary men and women who used it. It was their instrument of expression not alone for the things of every day, but with increasing eloquence for the things they thought and believed. The mass of the people were becoming articulate and learning to use the English language with passion and faith, with sorrow and courage, in defence of what they believed or fought for, in bitterness against their enemies, in comfort or exhortation to their friends. The language had become general from the Channel coast to the Scottish Lowlands and in scattered regions even farther north; it was spoken in Orkney, in much of Ross and Sutherland; it was the first language of the educated in Wales and was making progress even in Ireland.

The Celtic tongues, Gaelic and Welsh, were fast becoming the marks of barbarism; Cornish was dying on the lips of all but the fisher folk.

The talkative seventeenth century coincided with the confident and fertile youth of modern English. The structure of its grammar was still forming, the richness of its vocabulary still increasing; the clichés and the commonplaces were as yet few in number; professional jargon was limited. When Clarendon wrote his *History* and Walton his *Compleat Angler*, their brains were not clogged with the lees of other statesmen's memoirs or other rural reminiscences. The writers of the seventeenth century were not, of course, uninfluenced by the past. For the most part highly conscious of their art, they sought models in classical or foreign predecessors and sometimes among English ones. They weighed their words with artistic deliberation and imitated or influenced each other. But the adolescent vigour of the language gave them opportunities of

originality denied to their descendants. It opened up
pitfalls too, in which many of them perished.

Their literature is thus a series of experiments by
which the language was perfected as a literary instrument. When the century opens, the language has already
passed the barriers of mere dialect; it can rank fairly
as the tongue of a civilized people and an instrument of
subtle communication. With eloquent brevity, Mr. G.
M. Young has described how the English of Elizabeth
and Shakespeare came into being:

> In the fabric of English civilization few strands are of
> greater consequence than the tidal flux and reflux
> between London and the country. Books were sold in
> Paul's Churchyard to be read at Oxford and Cambridge,
> in the manor houses and the parsonages, and in no other
> way could a national literature have come into being.
> ... The Queen's English, when the Queen was young,
> hardly reached sixty miles from London—far enough
> to take in Oxford and Cambridge—and that, as the
> Spanish Ambassador once hinted, was about as far as
> her religion reached either. The English which we
> speak, our diction, grammar and rhythm, has I suppose
> its origins in the *lingua franca* of those three centres, carried
> about the country by judges and counsel on assize, by
> Parliament men sitting in Quarter Sessions, by preachers,
> by players, by the termers, law students in vacation.
> And, by the mid-Elizabethan time, I think we can say
> 'Here is at last a language, waiting only for a poet to
> teach it how to sing'.[1]

By 1600 more than one poet had taught the language
how to sing. But if England's greatest poet came
astoundingly, at the very outset, there was much still for
lesser men to do. When the century dawns word-making

[1] G. M. Young: *To-day and Yesterday*, pp. 279-80 (Rupert
Hart-Davis, London, 1948).

and phrase-making are in full flood, with John Florio, lexicographer, translator, and wordwright, hard at work, and the Authorized Version of the Bible, the greatest of all phrase-makers, eleven years in the future. Grammar was still, to many writers, a difficulty. When in doubt they looked to Latin or Italian, and tortured their straightforward, uninflected, essentially simple language on the rack of an alien grammar. The result is the alternate splendour and chaos of early seventeenth-century prose.

By mid-century the grammatical problems were mostly solved, the word-making slackened, the phrase-making grew less extravagant. Writers devoted themselves to acquiring elegance, flexibility, technique. The language of literature had stopped showing off and was learning the manners of the drawing-room. By 1700 it has added to the confidence of youth the confidence of breeding.

Two stages may be distinguished in the course of the century, the one arising out of the other by imperceptible degrees. English literature, like English politics, grew from deep roots and was continuous. Even in the drama, where the closing of the theatres during the Civil War is sometimes held to represent a break in tradition, the development in fact remained unbroken. Wycherley's *Love in a Wood* (1671) which takes place in St. James's Park, is only just across the way from Shirley's *Hide Park* (1632), and the same country breezes blow through Farquhar's *Recruiting Officer* (1706) as through Heywood's *Woman Killed with Kindness* a hundred years before.

There was loss as well as gain in the century's development. That was inevitable. It would be outside the scope of this book to consider the fate of the Celtic languages. Beaten back, like the Celtic peoples, by the triumphant onrush of English, they were passing through a period of decline and transition over which a partial darkness still hangs. Ian Lom and other Macdonald bards still, in the Western Highlands, sang the victories of their people, and in Ireland the story-tellers still rhythmically muttered their soporific tales to soothe the sleepless heads of their native chiefs, but Pierce Ferriter, the chief Irish poet of the time, perished at the hands of the English. In Wales, Rhys Pritchard sought in his religious poems *Cannwyll y Cymry* (*The Welshmen's Candle*) to naturalize the new English metres into the old Welsh tongue. Another decline was that of Scots-English, the last of the alternative Anglo-Saxon forms to capitulate to the English of the south. Abandoned by its educated men, it has few poets and no major writer between the end of the sixteenth century and its revival by Allan Ramsay in the eighteenth, though the anonymous writers of the ballads preserved its old tradition.

The English of the south became the King's English; but this did not mean that a single standard pronunciation yet existed. A broad accent was the mark of the uneducated and the butt of the mimic, but regional accents in a modified form were usual, and the uninhibited use of regional words and phrases gave vivacity to the written, as to the spoken, language.

The language was still new enough for its qualities and defects to be the object of technical argument between writers. The century opened with Thomas Campion's vigorous plea for blank verse, with a demonstration of the different rhythms and measures to which English words could be made to fit; he spoke no more than truth when he lamented the difficulty, among so many consonants, of 'giving the vowel convenient liberty'. The 'concourse of our monosyllables', he added, 'make our verses unapt to slide'. But monosyllables, as Sir John Beaumont declared in rhyme, have virtues of their own:

> Our Saxon shortness hath peculiar grace
> In choice of words fit for the ending place,
> Which leave impression in the mind as well
> As closing sounds of some delightful bell.

Another advantage of the language, as an earlier critic had pointed out, was the great number of ways in which a single idea could be expressed: 'For example when we would be rid of one, we use to say *Be going, trudge, pack, be faring, hence, away, shift*, and by circumlocution, *rather your room than your company, let's see your back, come again when I bid you, spare us your place, save your credit, the door is open for you, there's nobody holds you. . . .*'

The variety was, however, still not enough and foreign words were freely naturalized or dialect words exalted for general use. French was the chief and dominant source throughout the century, but the English had taken anything that caught their fancy: *portico, piazza, stanza,* and *garble* from the Italian; *cargo, cabal, embargo, grandee, armada, armadillo,* and *alligator* from the Spanish; *domineer* and *plunder* and *forlorn hope* from the Low and High Dutch; *canoe* and *cannibal* and *hurricane* and *tobacco* from the West Indians; *divan, dervish,* and *sultan* from the Turks; *rajah* and *nabob* from the Hindus.

The language had also maintained its old German capacity of making compound words for special meanings, a capacity very useful to the poets with their *cloud-capp'd, sky-born, whey-faced, white-livered, sin-sick,* and the rest. It was furthermore well suited to the invention of onomatopoeic words, a kind of verbal game in which the people took pleasure. Reiteration and alliteration created and perpetuated many a happy homely phrase: *flip-flap*, *clip-clop*, *hugger-mugger*, *higgledy-piggledy*, *tell-tale*, as well as the more immediately expressive *giggle*, *crackle*, and *crash*, and the slopping sound of *loblolly*, the seaman's phrase for his gruel.

Knotty Anglo-Saxon formed the muscle and sinews of a language grown at last supple with words from the latin tongues. It was still without abstract terms, the hideous 'isms' of philosophy and religion. Necessity was the mother of invention and this lack of abstracts compelled writers to invent concrete images to express general ideas. 'The Papacy is not other than the Ghost of the deceased Roman Empire, sitting crowned upon the grave thereof', wrote Hobbes, and fixed a grisly unforgotten picture.

Our ancestors in 1600 were unlike us in many ways. The phlegmatic Englishman had not yet become an established type. In 1600 the English were a lively, excitable, high-spirited people, expressing themselves spontaneously in song and rhyme, exclamation and gesture. They enjoyed acting, mumming, mimicry, country dances and round games, of which they had an unconscionable number, 'barley-break', 'John, come kiss me now', 'hot cockles', 'handy dandy', 'leap candle', and 'fair and softly passeth lent', the names tumble out of the old books with their suggestions of romp and laughter.

'Farewell rewards and fairies', lamented Bishop Corbet in his pleasant elegy for the country customs which he saw declining; but if some had already vanished many survived, superstitions and ancient rites, rush-bearings, wassails, and wakes. The influence of Puritanism, which by the end of the century had transformed middle-class life alike in town and country, had not yet penetrated into the fibres of society. 'Dost thou think, because thou art virtuous, there shall be no more cakes and ale? . . . Yes by Saint Anne, ginger shall be hot in the mouth too.' . . . Most Englishmen still joined with Sir Toby Belch in twitting the Puritan Malvolio. At Ben Jonson's Bartholomew Fair the gingerbread women and the costardmongers have the laugh of Zeal-of-the-land Busy with his unctuous disapproval.

Life was shorter, noisier, gayer, and more dreadful: shot with pain for which there was no help, and darkened by illnesses for which there was no cure. Society was indifferently fenced with political guarantees and administrative practice, through which in a hundred places disorder, oppression, and injustice could still break a way. Pestilence and famine killed their thousands each year.

The Citizens fled away, as out of a house on fire, and stuffed their pockets with their best ware, and threw themselves into the highways, and were not received, so much as into barns, and perished so, some of them with more money about them, than would have bought the village where they died. A Justice of the Peace . . . told me of one that died so, with £1400 about him.

This is not the Great Plague of 1665; it is another plague year, a bad one admittedly, about forty years earlier, described in a letter from John Donne. 'Can you dance the shaking of the sheets?' asked a grim little streetsong: meaning the marriage-night, or meaning death —sometimes the one and sometimes the other. With all the danger and the cruelty, the poverty and the pain, English life seems to have had the colour and the irrepressible gaiety now only found in warmer climates.

Out of this soil grew the prolific literature of the century. These were the crude surroundings among which its men of letters flourished. The more fortunate ones acquired their education in the thirty or forty great schools which taught the classics in the Renaissance manner, the less fortunate in the innumerable older-fashioned grammar schools where Christian authors were read for preference. As grown men they exchanged ideas in the universities and in London at the Inns of Court.

Alongside these casual nurseries of talent, there were the nurseries of criticism. In London, above all, there grew up in the course of the century the educated critical public whose opinions made or damned the writer: the *élite* of theatre audiences, the leisured middle and upper classes who read in their studies and talked literature in the parlour, and who, as the century went on, exerted their influence over literary fashion; gradually they transferred literary dispute to a wider and less professional sphere, from the taverns where the poets met and the booksellers' booths in Paul's Churchyard to the parks and the coffee-houses where the cultured strolled or sat and the wits displayed themselves. Language, literature, and critical public, all grew together.

The effect of political and even of social conditions on literature can be too curiously pursued. The eccentric and individual minds of writers do not necessarily echo every alteration in the surrounding world. The continuous careers of a great number both of major and minor writers bridge over the changes of the political and the social world. If Jonson belongs wholly to the first half of the century and Dryden to the second, what of Milton, Marvell, Cowley, Davenant, Waller, Denham, all of whom lived and wrote and consistently developed across

B

the confusion and changes of the mid-century? Too much can be made of the difference between one generation and the next. All ages are in reality ages of transition.

Yet the atmosphere of the century and the nature of its literary achievement does pass through certain recognizable phases. Queen Anne's Augustan Age seems a long century removed from the High Renaissance of Queen Elizabeth. In the opening twenty years of the seventeenth century there is still an atmosphere of blithe confidence, which breaks down little by little into the tentative anxiety, the slightly apologetic who-cares, who-knows attitude of the Caroline age, accompanied by an increase in introspection and moral earnestness whenever the lighter mood is abandoned. This lighter mood is the direct ancestor of Restoration cynicism, just as the moral earnestness is the ancestor of the steady gravity of the opposition writers. Thus in literature, as in politics, the seventeenth century saw the growth of a two-party system, Court and Opposition, light and serious. The seeds of the division are apparent as early as the time of Charles I; all that followed was the logical outcome.

These conceptions are, however, less important, in the study of literature, than the development of techniques and the manipulation of language. The great achievement of this century was to perfect English as a literary instrument, just as the political achievement was to develop (but not to perfect) the Parliamentary system as an instrument of government. In both achievements the insular character and stubborn vitality of the people was of some importance, for in literature as in politics outside influences, forcing the native genius in other directions, were persistent and strong.

We had a language and we had writers who managed

to assimilate, to resist, or to reject the pressure from Spain and Italy and France. Given the period, English literature might very well have been the merest hotchpotch of prevailing European rules and ideas. The powerful individuality of the writers of the time prevented this; even when they translated they went to conquer rather than to copy. Thus Chapman can write proudly of his *Odyssey*:

> Nor did the Argive ship more burthen feel,
> That bore the care of all men in her keel,
> Than my adventurous bark; the Colchian fleece
> Not half so precious as this soul of Greece,
> In whose songs I have made our shores rejoice,
> *And Greek itself vail to our English voice.*

He reveres this precious soul of Greece, as a translator should, but he sees nothing odd in suggesting that the Greek language must vail, or bow in reverence, to the English tongue. A little later in the century Christopher Harvey went further:

> Roman and Grecian muses, all give way;
> Our English poem darkens all your day.

Thus, too, of the perpetual robberies and plagiarisms of foreign subjects—their perpetrators always believed they had improved the originals; we may blush for the insensitive conceit of Wycherley announcing that he has (in his *Plain Dealer*) improved on Molière's *Le Misanthrope*; but the illusion was a healthy vanity. It preserved the English muse from slavish imitation and gave her a conceit of herself which, although it was not always justified in individual cases, was richly justified in general.

The root of it all was the love, amounting to infatuation, that nearly all these writers had for the English language.

Samuel Daniel, prophesying the greatness of his native tongue, was voicing a widespread contemporary opinion.

Or should we careless come behind the rest
In power of words, that go before in worth;
When as our accent's equal to the best,
Is able greater wonders to bring forth?
When all that ever hotter spirits expressed
Comes bettered by the patience of the North?
And who, in time, knows whither we may vent
The treasure of our tongue? To what strange shores,
This gain of our best glory shall be sent,
T' enrich unknowing nations with our stores?
What worlds in th' yet unformed Occident,
May come refin'd with th' accents that are ours?

Out of the blindness of love, he spoke truer than he knew. The beginning of great literature is always the love of language, for itself, in itself. English, now to so many writers a wife to whom, for better for worse, they have long been bound, was to the men of the seventeenth century, a still mysterious, still unconquered mistress.

CHAPTER II

THE JACOBEAN AGE: PROSE

WITHIN THE first fourteen years of the century Florio translated Montaigne, Raleigh wrote his *History of the World,* and the Authorized Version of the Bible was published. The last of these three may appear at first to be the most evidently influential. Yet the influence of the Bible on English prose style, idioms apart, has been much exaggerated.

This was fortunate, for the Authorized Version owes its unique qualities to characteristics which would have made it, as a literary model, disastrous. The translators of the Bible were the antithesis of Chapman; they had no intention of making Greek or Hebrew 'vail to our English voice'. They did not set out, like most of the great translators of the period, to recreate as an *English* masterpiece the foreign text before them. They set out, with their detailed scholarship and improved knowledge, to revise the so-called Bishops' Bible of 1568, collating it with other English translations, notably the wonderfully vigorous version of Tyndale and the Geneva version prepared by English refugees under Calvinist auspices. They produced, therefore, a text which is beautiful indeed, but which is couched in language deliberately archaic and has the impersonality inevitable in a scholarly work of synthesis. Although Tyndale's work is often the basis of the Authorized Version, its

15

compilers sacrificed, along with his highly personal and tendentious marginal notes, also the colloquial tang of his style. Joseph, in the Authorized Version, is no longer described as a 'lucky fellow' because the Lord was with him.

Their language was thus a century out of date in 1611, and was drained of those brisk, concrete, personal touches which were typical of the natural, native prose of England. What the Authorized Version gained, besides a greater accuracy, was a peculiar, impersonal dignity. It was easy to believe that this English Bible was a divinely inspired book.

The translators, however, not only adopted the archaic style of the last century; they respected the verbal inspiration of the original so deeply that they translated idiomatic phrases word for word, a habit which makes often for an unearthly grandeur and mystery but sometimes for mere confusion. John Selden, eminent as a scholar and as a man of good sense, regretted that God's word should have been made so difficult for the multitude of simple Englishmen:

There is no book so translated as the Bible: . . . if I translate a French book into English, I turn it into English phrase, not French English. *Il fait froid*: I say *'tis cold*, not *it makes cold*: but the Bible is rather translated into English words than into English phrase. The Hebraisms are kept, and the phrase of that language is kept . . . which is well enough so long as scholars have to do with it, but, when it comes among the common people, Lord, what gear do they make of it?

What the common people, oddly enough, made of this gear was a host of new phrases. The crockets of this prodigious anonymous edifice were broken off in handfuls to ornament the living-rooms of the spoken language.

'Black but comely', 'the eleventh hour', 'the fat of the land', 'a lordly dish', 'no mean city', 'the shadow of death', 'a howling wilderness'—by little and little the people carried them away and embedded them in their talk, with one or two outlandish place-names, too, that had nothing to do with any country they had ever seen— 'the fleshpots of Egypt', 'the waters of Babylon', 'the rose of Sharon', 'the hosts of Midian'.

There were other strange effects; one Hebrew idiom at least acquired a mysterious splendour on the tongues of the English, and it is with difficulty even now that we realize that the Ancient of Days is no more than an idiom meaning 'old'. As for Adam's Eve created as 'a help meet for him', 'helpmeet' she became, and helpmeet she obstinately persisted on a million vulgar tongues until the King's English and the Dictionary gave in and a new word was added to the language.

Insidious and diffused, an influence extending over the whole country, the effect of the Authorized Version on the spoken language eludes any exact estimation. Milton grafts Biblical words with sonorous accuracy into his classical sentences; Bunyan's simple, colloquial prose is thick with recollected phrases. The profound effect of Biblical reading is felt in the ideas and thought of almost all the serious writers of the century and may be traced in part to the official distribution of the Authorized Version. But it should be remembered that the Puritans for two or three generations after 1611 continued to prefer the text of the Geneva Bible. As to style, the tough and fertile English prose of the day grew into its own personal, idiosyncratic, or conventional shapes with a healthy disregard for the rich, archaic, foreign-sounding sentences flowing every Sunday from the lectern.

The influence of Florio or of Raleigh was of quite a different quality, and strictly confined to the educated and to literature. John Florio is one of the most attractive and amusing figures of English literary history. Italian by extraction, although born and bred a Londoner, he enjoyed a snug appointment at Court as foreign reader to King James's Queen, Anne of Denmark. He was a character and something of a fantastic, above all a great lover of words. His Italian dictionary, pleasantly titled *A World of Words*, bears eloquent witness alike to his love and his knowledge. He is rarely content with one English version but commonly provides two or three for every Italian word, proving, if proof were needed, the variety and flexibility of his vocabulary in his adopted tongue. Thus 'arrancare' is 'to hurle or twirle about. Also to goe or trudge or skud away in haste'; and the onomatopoeic 'sussurare' has some pretty equivalents: 'to whisper, to mutter or murmure. Also to humme or buzze as Bees. Also to charme or forespeake with whispring words. Also to make a low, a soft or still noise as a gentle winde among trees, or a gentle-gliding streame among pible-stones, or as birds chirping and chattring among woods.'

It is odd that this excitable little man should have been attracted by the meticulous, contemplative, detached mind of Montaigne; perhaps he recognized in him a writer as loquacious as himself. His translation is far more than a great translation; it is an independent contribution to literature. For a more exact rendering of the French original there is the later work of Charles Cotton. But the Florio-Montaigne combination remains inimitable: the French dish with the Italian sauce which by so odd a chance appears on the English bill of fare.

Florio is sometimes, but not often, wide of the mark; in general Montaigne's placid recordings are accurately rendered in meaning but, sentence by sentence, subtly fantasticated. The musing gentleman and his four-square château which seem, in the French, to merge with the unobtrusive landscape of central France, stand out in the English with an uncanny brilliance of detail. It is as though a picture in water-colours had been enthusiastically copied in enamel.

Florio's work had a twofold effect on English prose writers. His translation of Montaigne introduced them to the leisurely, human style of writing and to the rambling personal essay which writers from Cowley onwards were to make into so fertile a province of English literature. His indefatigable work as interpreter and lexicographer demonstrated conclusively that English could vie even with the admired Italian language for a rich, expressive, and varied vocabulary.

Randle Cotgrave's French-English Dictionary (1611) was another valuable influence on the vocabulary of the educated. Among translators, Philemon Holland, the 'Translator Generall' as Fuller called him, was steadily demonstrating—without Florio's eccentricity—the capacity of English for capturing the sense and atmosphere of classical prose.

Sir Walter Raleigh's style was neither showy nor eccentric, and his influence on later writers and his literary achievement have been rather under than over-rated. During his long imprisonment in the Tower he evolved what may fairly be called 'historian's prose'. His *History of the World* was read with pleasure and profit by generation after generation in the seventeenth century. He was widely quoted and widely recommended; Oliver Cromwell sought to induce a taste for him in his son Richard, and the youthful Montrose treasured the *History*. The echo of that clear, impressive style is to be heard time and again on the lips of orators in Parliament, in the letters of public men, in Clarendon and even in the debased Burnet.

Raleigh who, like most of his contemporaries, regarded classical writers, and classical orators, as the most suitable models, uses a sentence-structure which is often too long for English. But his natural ear and his desire for clarity above all enabled him to fashion these lengthy sentences into an easy, dignified prose that would serve alike for narrative, reflection, and argument. He was the first to create what was later to become the special facility of English historians, the faculty for mingling sound historical narrative with intelligent general reflections and parenthetical argument.

In making his *History of the World* a demonstration of God's judgements on the wicked, he was merely following a fashion common among European historians since St. Augustine had compelled world history in his *City of God* to yield a religious moral. But Raleigh, with an explorer's interest in finding things out, a scholar's conscience, and a captive's interminable leisure created an unusually effective synthesis between history, philosophy, and moral instruction which is moreover artistically satisfying. His facts may not always be correct, but he had done his best to make them so, which is the most that any historian can do, and he tells them plainly, giving full weight to their intrinsic interest. His philosophical reflections are never out of place, and his most brilliant phrases—he had been a courtier in the heyday of Elizabethan word-play and repartee—are never too glittering for the context. He inserts his epigrams with unobtrusive ease and can write 'It is not truth but opinion that can travel the world without a pass-port' so naturally that it does not jump out of the paragraph. His famous and much quoted climax—the lines begin- ing 'O eloquent, just, and mighty Death'—is a climax indeed, but the way towards it is slowly and carefully prepared and it legitimately ends a chapter.

His book was especially popular among the Puritans and those opposed to the Court. The manner of his death as a victim of the King's unpopular foreign policy had something to do with this, but his treatment of monarchs in the *History*, described by the King's friends as 'too saucy' also in part accounts for it. He saw the great of this world in their petty proportion against time and eternity, and he would allow to no one a whit more than his due. His morality is sound, but it supplied examples that did not tally with the theory of Divine Right. His dismissal of Alexander the Great is typical :

For his person, it is very apparent that he was as valiant as any man—a disposition, taken by itself, not much to be admired; for I am confident that he had ten thousand in his army as daring as himself. Surely, if adventurous natures were to be commended simply, we should confound that virtue with the hardiness of thieves, ruffians, and mastiff dogs; for certainly it is noways praiseworthy but in doing good things.

The most distinguished exponent of formal prose at this time was Francis Bacon. His *Essays*, first issued in 1597 and re-issued with numerous additions during the next twenty-five years, are the beautifully wrought work of a late Renaissance artist, using all the rules of imagery, contrast, and balance set down by the Italian rhetoricians, to produce an effect at once elegant, dignified, and rich. Quotations from the *Essays*, whose philosophy is as worldly and Renaissance as the style, have become proverbial; his sentences have the impersonality, the anonymity, but not the rusticity, of proverbs.

He that will apply new remedies must expect new evils; for time is the greatest innovator.

All rising to great place is by a winding stair.

His *History of Henry VII* has greater warmth and fluency. This book, which was an apologia for James I fairly heavily disguised in a learned account of the reign of the first of the Tudors, probably contains much of what Bacon felt and hoped to teach about the practice of politics. But it is significant that when his intention was to write for posterity, he preferred Latin to his own language. He turned the superb English of his *Advancement of Learning* into Latin for its definitive version. If this was not exactly unusual in the opening years of the seventeenth century it places Bacon nevertheless among those who distrusted the permanent qualities of English. It is not really surprising that, although his English prose will always give the pleasure that a finished artistry must convey, it does not belong to the organic part of our literature.

Unlike Bacon, Robert Burton, fellow of Christ Church and rector of Segrave, decided to use English as the vehicle for his far-reaching and profound inquiry into the vagaries of the human mind. His *Anatomy of Melancholy* ran into five editions between its publication in 1621 and his death in 1640. This was partly a tribute to the remarkable penetration of his analysis, but the book was also extremely entertaining.

Melancholy—a broad term covering a great number of mental diseases, more especially the hysterical and hallucinatory—gave Burton his connecting thread for a book into which he methodically crammed the miscellaneous anecdotal gleanings of his reading and his life. He had perused medical and herbal treatises, theological works of all kinds, poetry, philosophy, and history, classical and contemporary. Within the ingeniously plotted headings into which he divides his subject, he is abundantly discursive. He finds no difficulty, for instance, in introducing his social reflections on the English gentry, a celebrated passage from which Macaulay later borrowed some details.

The major part . . . are wholly bent for hawks and hounds, and carried away many times with intemperate lust, gaming and drinking. If they read a book at any time . . . 'tis an English Chronicle, Sir Huon of Bordeaux, Amadis de Gaul, a play-book or some pamphlet of News, and that at such seasons only, when they cannot stir abroad; to drive away time, their sole discourse is dogs, hawks, hounds and what news? If some one have been a traveller in Italy, or as far as the Emperor's Court, wintered in Orleans, and can court his mistress in broken French, wear his clothes nearly in the newest fashion, sing some choice outlandish tunes, discourse of lords, ladies, towns, palaces, and cities, he is complete and to be admired.

Topography always interested the inquiring, practical minds of the seventeenth century. Raleigh had speculated on the location of Paradise; Burton speculated, and quoted authorities, on the location of Hell. 'Lessius', he writes, 'will have this local Hell . . . one Dutch mile in diameter, all filled with fire and brimstone: because, as he there demonstrates, that space cubically multiplied will make a Sphere able to hold eight hundred thousand millions of damned bodies (allowing each body six foot square) which will abundantly suffice.'

It is difficult to place this book solemnly on its literary merits. It is a work of impressive and genuine scholarship, of which the style conveys at once to the reader the enthusiasm and the charm of the author. Burton's sentences seem to tumble headlong out of his richly furnished mind and tend, moreover, to rush from English into Latin and from Latin into English like a train going through a series of tunnels. But he says what he means, without art, and in spite of the Latin quotations —so natural to a don—he can be regarded as the first and still one of the best of our talkative writers. The reader is aware all the time of the author's tone of voice, now gay, now mocking, now good-humoured, occasionally reproachful, with intimate and courteous touches like the metaphorical bow which he pauses to make to 'Mr. Otho Nicholson, founder of our waterworks and elegant conduit in Oxford'. Among later English writers in the talkative manner, Laurence Sterne and Charles Lamb both owed much to him.

The novel, which had begun well before the close of Elizabeth's reign with such works of roguery and adventure as Nash's *Unfortunate Traveller,* was now, for a long period, almost to disappear. Light readers were content—as Burton contemptuously pointed out—with *Huon of Bordeaux* and *Amadis of Gaul,* to which old tales of daring, love, and chivalry might be added *Palmerin of England, Guy of Warwick,* and Montemayor's *Diana.* A more fashionable or more intelligent public was pleased with *Don Quixote,* excellently done into English by Shelton in 1612, or—a turn for the worse—with that asphyxiating pastoral romance from France, Honoré d' Urfé's *Astrée*, whose volumes began to appear in 1607. There were also, for the novelty-seeking public, the play-books of the dramas which had pleased London audiences or perhaps been presented 'with applause' before the King's Majesty.

Among connoisseurs, however, a new kind of prose amusement came into vogue about this time. This was the 'Character'. The idea was borrowed from the Greek philosopher, Theophrastus, who had written short pieces illustrating human qualities. Joseph Hall's collection of *Characters*, which closely follows the Theophrastan type, appeared in 1608. The idea soon took hold with the dilettanti of the Inns of Court, the universities, and the taverns, among whom small descriptive paragraphs were soon being lovingly and wittily composed and circulated for admiration in manuscript. Very soon the Character ceased to be the personification of some vice or virtue, and grew into a careful or pregnant observation of a social type—an Hypocrite, a Courtier, a Roaring Boy. Sometimes even a well-known public figure would be attempted under the transparent veil of a type.

The publication of the so-called Overburian characters in 1614 confirmed this new development. Sir Thomas Overbury, something of a character himself, vain, witty, and accomplished, had been murdered in the course of a Court intrigue. He had written before he died perhaps half a dozen of these Characters. His work was now printed together with a good many more pieces written by his friends and contemporaries. The popularity of this book, and the publicity which came to its author when the King's favourite, Robert Carr, was tried for his murder, caused it to run into several later and expanded editions. Thirty-two Characters, almost certainly from the hand of the dramatist John Webster, were among those added later. The hand of Dekker has been detected in others.

But if professionals were from time to time called in by publishers to fill out a popular volume, the Characters remained amateurs' pieces *par excellence*. Their authorship, even when the pieces were collected under one name, was usually various and is often difficult to establish with certainty. The exercise was later extended, as in Wye Saltonstall's collection, to cover places as well as persons. As an educated amusement it went on for the whole of a generation, adding a number of pleasantly memorable paragraphs to the sum total of English literature, as well as much that has only antiquarian interest. The character of a child, from the *Microcosmographie* which is attributed to John Earle, is a pretty example of the Character at its lightest:

His soul is yet a white paper, unscribbled with observations of the world, wherewith, at length, it becomes a blurred notebook. He is purely happy, because he knows no evil, nor hath made means by sin to be acquainted with misery. . . . We laugh at his foolish sports, but his game is our earnest; and his drums, rattles and hobby-horses, but the emblems and mocking of men's business. . . . Could he put off his body with his little coat, he had got eternity without a burden, and exchanged but one heaven for another.

The value of such writing, practised over a long period and by many writers, was that of an exercise. The composition of Characters taught curious and careful observation and encouraged amateur writers to consider the intrinsic and allusive value of their words. Such an outburst of exercising proves how general and how serious was the interest in writing in the early part of the century.

With this interest in writing and in language went an energetic interest in life. The hurly-burly of the capital, the tricks of the confidence men, the oaths of the bravos, the cant of beggars and vagabonds—all had their students. A whole literature of roguery was already growing up. Dekker, the indefatigable dramatist of London life, compiled in *Lanthorn and Candlelight* an early glossary of thieves' language. Coney-catching pamphlets, descriptions and warnings of the danger lying in wait for the country coneys, the rabbits, who ventured up to town, were popular, and written with as much enjoyment as knowledge. Samuel Rowlands's racy dialogues between different familiar city types show the same faculty for general observation, the same interest in the comedy and reality of life. These lively characteristics run through English light literature from Chaucer to the present day.

Books of travel, immensely popular in this age of expansion, had started brilliantly with Hakluyt's collection of *Voyages*. This was continued into the seventeenth century by Samuel Purchas in *Purchas his Pilgrimes*. To these authentic tales of exploration and discovery belongs also John Smith's vigorous account of his experiences in Virginia and elsewhere. He was a man of a vivid pen and a coloured imagination, but his book is substantially based on fact. Elsewhere the true, the false, and the farcical are richly combined : in such works as the Somerset-born Tom Coryate's *Crudities*, or the Scot, William Lithgow's *Painful Peregrinations* with their highly coloured pictures of Turkish baths or Venetian magnificence. A kind of alert simplicity illumines the pages of

c

another loquacious traveller, John Taylor, the 'water poet', who, when he was not scribbling doggerel or trying to circumnavigate England in a boat made of stiffened paper, composed two excellent accounts, one of a visit to Scotland, and another of a tour through Germany.

A new kind of direct prose may be seen emerging in such of these works as were not intended for a purely literary audience. The same increasingly direct style was also being evolved by the many writers of social and practical handbooks in which the period abounded; such works as Peacham's *Compleat Gentleman*, Brathwaite's *English Gentleman*, or Markham's *Country Contentments*. These books were not always conscious literature, and sometimes not literature at all, but they were in time to have a significant influence on the development and simplification of English prose.

There was still in the earlier part of the century a clear distinction between the literary and the colloquial language, a distinction which, while classical models were copied, was bound to cripple the development of an easy native style in prose. An ambitious young man, with a political career ahead of him, would at this time compose speeches for practice in the manner of Seneca or Cicero. Where the orator could impose on these models a natural eloquence and an extensive English vocabulary, the result might be very striking;[1] more often, it was cramped and artificial.

It is perhaps in the surviving letters of the period that this conflict can be most interestingly traced. Letters, among the cultured, were regarded as works of art in which grace and elegance were of more importance than

[1] Strafford, whose eloquence is quoted in a later chapter, taught himself by this method.

spontaneity. Those who had no literary gift, or in-
sufficient time always to exercise it, sometimes had their
letters drafted and composed for them. Secretaries of
State were truly secretaries in the sense that an accomplished epistolary style was expected of them. In a lower
sphere of society Complete Letter-Writers were much
in demand, *A Pattern for Pen-men* being an especially
popular handbook. James Howell's *Epistolae Ho-elianae*
remains an attractive classic of the mannered style of
letter-writing.

But the letters of two leading diplomats of the period,
Sir Henry Wotton and Sir Dudley Carleton, show already
that personality and spontaneity could be achieved
without sacrifice of elegance. These two men, both
learned scholars, both men of wide reading, managed to
convey the warm humour of their own personalities,
with many an acute touch of observation, while yet
scarcely breaking out of the ornate framework of the
literary letter. The full triumph of the spontaneous
letter was to be for a later generation.

The high stronghold of mannered prose was still the
pulpit. Churchgoing was compulsory (in theory) and
the congregations in London at least were likely to be as
critical of preachers as they were of players. The
great sermons, preached on special occasions, were
events to which connoisseurs looked forward. Lancelot
Andrewes, the most famous preacher of the early years
of the century, is, after a long eclipse, returning to-day
into the favour of the discriminating few. His manner
must, however, have depended much on the sweet and
persuasive delivery which earned him the epithet 'silver-
tongued'. His technique was to subdivide his text into
small particles—the practice that George Herbert was

later to condemn as 'crumbling a text'—and then to ruminate on each part of it. The result is a staccato, parenthetical style, often very difficult to follow, but rewarding for those who can acquire the taste, for the mind of Andrewes was a lofty and penetrating one.

The sermons of the most famous preacher of the next decade, John Donne, whose prose is not altogether to be divided from his poetry, are very different from those of Andrewes. There is here no anatomizing of the text, but instead a compelling, dark, and difficult eloquence, a mixture of medieval logic with the sensual speculation of the Renaissance. This unresolved conflict is typical of the religious outlook of the age, in which the orthodoxy of a recent past conflicted with the explosive heterodoxy of the present. Above this mental and emotional chaos, Donne is conscious of a supreme power in whose hand order lies and against whom all argument is vain.

Poor intricated soul! Riddling, perplexed, labyrinthical soul! Thou couldest not say, that thou believest not in God, if there were no God; thou couldest not believe in God, if there were no God; if there were no God, thou couldest not speak, thou couldest not think, not a word, not a thought, no not against God. . . .

This inescapable and terrible God is the constant figure of Donne's universe.

We cannot ceil the Heavens with a roof of brass, but that God can come down in thunder that way, nor pave the earth with a floor of brass, but that God can come up in earthquake that way.

An unrelenting God overhung the ant-heap activities of men, their ineffective protests, and their bold speculations. In the course of the century this figure was to recede from the consciousness of one part of society at least. But the first half of the seventeenth century was perhaps the most profoundly and thoughtfully religious in English experience since the Middle Ages. Its literature and its politics are saturated with religious conviction and in part inspired by them. It is the lack of a profound religious sense in Francis Bacon which makes his writing, in style, so essentially of the Renaissance. It is the sense of the presence of God which makes Sir Walter Raleigh in his writings so much a man of the seventeenth century.

The growth of scientific knowledge was not at first in conscious opposition to the religious outlook. Indeed the two went for a long period in close alliance; the germ of the Royal Society (founded in 1660) was in the meetings during the Civil War of inquirers who, while repudiating the bitter conflict over religion, remained themselves devout believers. Among the earliest Fellows of the Society, Robert Boyle and John Evelyn were outstandingly zealous and active Christians. But it was inevitable that, as the century advanced and the religious hopes of both Anglicans and Puritans were destroyed in a long war, the scientific and enlightened outlook should become identified with a conventional or indifferent attitude to religion. The brooding presence of God had withdrawn from polite literature by the end of the century. It remained, all the more powerful for being thus restricted, as the inspiration of a sectarian literature.

The struggle of the Puritan outlook for domination over all society ended in defeat as far as the capital, the upper class, and polite literature were concerned. But it did not end in total defeat; the bulk of the middle classes remained under this powerful—and often inspiring—spell. The effect which this division was to have on the future of English literature is already foreshadowed by the end of the seventeenth century.

But in the first quarter of the century there is still a marked consistency of outlook, masqued only by variations of style. John Donne was unique in his eloquence and in his manner, but his outlook is typical. His dread of the living God and his fascination with his own soul and the nature of the physical world are characteristic of his epoch. Two worlds which were bound to destroy each other—the one of faith, the other of inquiry—co-existed for a short while within the 'perplexed, labyrinthical' souls of the men of the Jacobean age.

CHAPTER III

THE JACOBEAN AGE: DRAMA

THE DISTINCTION between commercial and uncommercial writing is usually held to reflect discredit on the former. A 'pot-boiler', a 'commercial proposition'—these are not terms of praise in literature. Very little of the literature described in the last chapter was in any sense commercial; the Jacobean drama was nothing else.

The stage lived on the suffrages of the London citizens and apprentices, of the young country gentlemen from the Inns of Court, and the occasional courtiers who filled the benches of the 'wooden O' or hired themselves stools on the projecting apron stage itself. To this ravenous public, two playhouses [1] day in, day out, threw five-act comedies of love and intrigue and five-act tragedies of love and revenge. The turnover of the audience cannot have been large even in a town boasting London's hundred thousand souls. It had to be a different play as often as possible; a run of as much as five consecutive performances of the same piece was, in the first half of the century, phenomenal. Before this greedy, critical, uproarious crowd were poured out the jewels of an epoch richer in dramatic talent than any that has succeeded it.

Shakespeare must be left aside. His transcendent genius defies brief analysis, and it would be merely

[1] Before the closing of the theatres in 1642 the number had trebled.

absurd to affix to him such a label as Elizabethan or
Jacobean dramatist. Yet it is worth pondering the amaz-
ing truth that his works were written in the rough and
tumble of a commercial theatre and for spectators who
wolfed them down in an afternoon with the same coarse
relish as they wolfed all his contemporaries; two-thirds
of them appreciated the bear-baiting or the public
executions quite as much. It is true that, beyond the
walls of the playhouse, there was all over the country
a secondary audience, the reading public. These
devoured the playbooks and pored over the printed
page, assessing the verse and criticizing the plot, although
they had rarely seen a play performed. But success or
failure was first decided by the London audience, and
the country readers preferred to study a piece of which
the noisy fame had already reached them.

The dramatists who supplied the theatres wrote for
their living and for their public. But nearly all were
talented and one or two were men of genius who tore
their gifts to shreds in the struggle to satisfy the demand.
Some, like Webster and Chapman, had the stuff of great
poetry in them; some, like Heywood and Dekker and
Marston and, later, Shirley and Brome, had keen ears
for dialogue and a feeling for the humour of the common-
place and topical; some, like Fletcher and Middleton,
Massinger and Ford, had unusual insight into the human
mind. Almost all had a remarkable sense of the theatre
and great vitality.

They took their plots with both hands from Painter's
Palace of Pleasure, Fenton's *Certaine Tragicall Discourses*,
Belleforest's *Histoires Tragiques*, and other useful collec-
tions of romantic fables or scandals based on fact.
Giovanna of Naples became Webster's *Duchess of Malfi*,

Vittoria Accorombona the Victoria Corombona of his *White Devil*, Bianca Capella the strangely misprinted Brancha of Middleton's *Women beware Women*. Fable or scandal, fact or fiction, they dressed their stories up to suit their public—the tragedies with murder, suicide, and sudden death, the comedies with topical jokes, knock-about, and bawdry, both with plot and counterplot and sub-plot. They collaborated with each other and re-touched each other's works with a good nature that is the despair of textual critics. Beaumont and Fletcher, Fletcher and Middleton, Fletcher, Rowley and Ford, Heywood and Rowley, Dekker and Massinger, Mas-singer and Fletcher, Jonson, Marston and Chapman—all these combinations and more occur; even so there are orphan plays without discovered parentage.

Criticism, yet in its childhood, was immediate and noisy: the prologues asking for a hearing, and the epi-logues pleading for approval were not empty formalities. But—although Ben Jonson boldly and vainly tried—no one in England had yet turned drama into an academic study, urged the seemliness of the three unities, objected to the mixture of prose and verse, comedy and tragedy, naturalism and convention within a single play, or pro-tested that death itself, let alone stabbing, strangulation, and suicide, should occur with decency off stage and be known to the audience only by report.[1]

Stage conventions are often unaccountable. The twentieth century, while demanding the utmost natural-ism in production in the commercial drama, for many years agreed to the peculiar convention that murder frequently occurred among the upper classes. The

[1] The rule in classical and neo-classical drama.

peculiarities of the thriller are no odder in our time than those of the Jacobean drama were in theirs. Criticism of the plots of these dramatists on the score of improbability goes wide of the target; Jacobean audiences did not believe that the disguises and coincidences of the stage were *possible*, but they agreed to suspend disbelief because of the additional dramatic pleasure to be derived from so doing.

The output of plays in the first forty years of this century was prodigious; even the surviving output fills many shelves, and much, we know, has perished. Students of the English drama still curse the name of John Warburton, that rather disreputable antiquary of the eighteenth century who collected manuscripts of unpublished plays, but failed to keep them under lock and key so that his cook, Betsy Baker, used fifty-five and a half out of a total of fifty-nine for lighting the fire and lining her pie dishes. In spite of Betsy Baker, between two and three hundred plays have survived from the harvest-time of English drama before the theatres were closed in 1642 and the actors went off, the younger to the wars, the older to set up as ale-house keepers.

Several rough divisions of period and style may be imposed on this crowded half-century of production. Shakespeare, and more especially the lyrical-pastoral Shakespeare, sets the fashion as the century opens.[1] The next dominating theatrical influence is that of Ben Jonson with his rampageous comedies of humours with their full-blooded type-characterizations. When Jonson's

---

[1] Milton's phrase 'warbling his native wood-notes wild' rather aptly underlines the aspect of Shakespeare's genius which was most popular in his own time and in the period immediately following.

energies were diverted elsewhere, the prolific, good-humoured Fletcher long presided over the English stage, a genial, humane dramatist, whether in comedy or tragedy, lightly satirical in his comedies of manners, concerned in his tragedies with the human heart, rather than with the grandeurs of history. The opening years of Charles I belong to Philip Massinger, a historical-political dramatist, who was usually concerned with the problems of the moment, a preacher and a propagandist. The last period of all is James Shirley's. This inferior but prolific writer alternated between a kind of Shakespeare-and-sugar-water pastoral style and a highly developed comedy of manners in which all the seeds of Restoration Drama are already present.

These were the leaders only; among the rank and file marched many men with names as memorable. Among so rich a treasure the selection of single dramatists must depend on the caprice of the critic. Dekker, an acute student of phrase and idiom, developed an individual technique in handling London subjects. He was most at home with apprentices and craftsmen and his best-known play, *The Shoemaker's Holiday*, is as fresh and lively to-day as when it was written. Simon Eyre, the master shoe-maker, his good-hearted domineering wife and houseful of apprentices abound in life. The pathetic under-plot which tells of a young shoemaker who comes home disabled from the wars to find that his wife has disappeared but traces her at last when her wedding shoes come to him for repair, is, for all its surface improbability, true to the suffering of the inarticulate poor.

John Webster, on the strength of his lightning flashes of poetry and his powerful sense of theatre, will always be placed high among the Jacobean dramatists. His classical play, *Appius and Virginia*, is a failure, but *The White Devil* and *The Duchess of Malfi* still hold the stage. Both are based on Italian scandals; both are admirable theatre. The trial scene in *The White Devil* is outstanding as sheer drama; so is the crucial moment in *The Duchess of Malfi* where the Duchess, to avert suspicion, stages the public dismissal of the steward whom she deeply loves and to whom she is secretly married. The strangling of Duke Brachiano in *The White Devil* by his enemies, disguised as holy monks come to soothe his sick-bed, is a scene to make the flesh creep. 'This is a true love knot, sent from the Duke of Florence,' snarls one of these ghostly comforters as he slips the noose round the neck of the prostrate invalid. Webster's poetry has moments of a violent vision peculiarly attractive to our own violent time:

> My soul, like to a ship in a black storm,
> Is driven, I know not whither.

or

> Your brother and yourself are worthy men,
> You have a pair of hearts are hollowed graves.

In spite of this he hardly matches Beaumont and Fletcher, Massinger, or Middleton in the treatment of character, his tragedy has not the simple majesty of Chapman, and he lacks the dreadful insight of Ford into the abysses of the doomed soul. Beaumont is probably best remembered for that engaging comedy of London manners, *The Knight of the Burning Pestle*. His most celebrated serious play is *The Maid's Tragedy*. The poetic quality of the play is less remarkable than the ambitious and elaborate character study of the heroine, the scheming woman Evadne, who marries the Maid's betrothed, only to tell him on the wedding night that she is already the King's mistress. The plot is often clumsy, but the predicament of Evadne, a passionate woman tormented by the belated prickings of conscience, is wonderfully conveyed. Chapman, who couched his themes from French history in sombrely splendid verse, makes a figure of titanic tragedy out of the ambitious Duke of Biron who conspired against Henri IV.

Middleton, a writer nearly as prolific as Fletcher, had a wonderfully quick eye for women's psychology, all the more remarkable when we remember that he depended on the epicene presentations of these parts by twelve-year-old boys. In *The Changeling* he created not only a convincing villain, a creature of corrupting evil, in de Flores but also a convincing woman to be corrupted by him. Beatrice-Joanna is an intelligent animal creature, amoral because the sheltered life of a Renaissance woman has made her so; in order to escape a loveless marriage she sets on her devoted slave de Flores to kill her betrothed. She does not realize, a common feminine error, that devoted slaves can become tyrannous masters. The awakening is terrible. De Flores, fresh from murder, requires her to be his mistress. 'A woman dipp'd in blood, and talk of modesty!' he derides her, and when she urges her rank as a barrier to his suggestion:

Pish! Fly not to your birth, but settle you
In what the act has made you; you're no more
   now.
You must forget your parentage to me;
You are the deed's creature; . . .

Her agitated wiles to maintain the appearance of respectability exhaust and corrupt her and there is an agony almost of relief in her final exposure and death.

Jacobean society was still hierarchic, if no longer rigidly so. The colloquy between de Flores and Beatrice-Joanna would have needed no underlining to the audience of the day. Her assumption that her rank still placed her out of his reach and his suggestion that her rank has been discounted by her deed represent a common assumption and a common political argument of the time.

The hierarchy of society creates both the morality and the humour of many of the London comedies, and comedies set in London and depicting London life were increasingly popular up to the closing of the theatres. Thus in *Eastward Ho!*, a collaborative play on which Ben Jonson, Chapman, and Marston all seem to have worked, the merchant's wife is set on marrying her daughter to a knight and encourages the girl to boast of the social precedence she will thus enjoy, even over her mother. 'I must be a lady tomorrow,' says the girl, 'and by your leave, mother (I speak not without my duty, but only in the right of my husband) I must take place of you, mother.' 'That you shall, my daughter,' crows the foolish mother.

This exulting of the parents in the elevation of a child to the higher social sphere whither it is impossible for them to follow is touched with a more vehement hand both in Massinger's *City Madam* and yet more powerfully in his most famous play *A New Way to Pay Old Debts*. Massinger was politically opposed to the Court, but levelling doctrines had not yet reached the theatre, and he was firmly convinced of the rightness of the social hierarchy. In his philosophy those who try to break down the barriers of rank are either very foolish or very wicked. However limited his outlook, the human observation with which he sustains it is impressive. Thus the money-lender, Sir Giles Overreach, speaking to his daughter, gloats in advance over the joys that will be his when she has married a peer of the realm and he himself will have to enter her presence hat in hand:

> . . . think what 'tis
> For me to say, *My honourable daughter.*
> And thou, when I stand bare, to say 'Put on',
> Or 'Father, you forget yourself'.

This savage comedy is generally accounted Massinger's best play, and indeed Overreach himself is a gigantic and terrible figure that comes straddling out of the stage larger than life.

Massinger's more usual vein was romantic tragedy, although here, too, on a less satirical note, he was something of a moralist and something of a politician. While Sir Giles Overreach is undoubtedly intended as a caricature of a typical financier-adventurer with one or two personal side-glances at Sir Giles Mompesson, who had recently been impeached by Parliament for his malpractices, the political allusions in the tragedies are rather more obscure. King Charles personally deleted an oblique attack on Ship-money from one of his manuscripts. Good dramatist and good poet though Massinger was, he would have been very much at home in any period when the stage could be used as a vehicle for propaganda, social, moral, or political.

A certain moral intent is to be found in a good many of the social comedies of London life. Both Middleton's *A Trick to Catch the Old One* and Marston's *Dutch Courtesan*

draw conclusions about the excesses of youth, although
Middleton's moral is directed rather against the unsympathetic, elderly, and virtuous, Marston's against the
young and wild. The railing scene between the Dutch
courtesan and her bawd when she believes she has lost
her lover has the authentic tang of a dialogue overheard
in Blackfriars, but Marston's comic vein tends to a
certain harshness which suggests that his talent might
have mellowed better with more cosseting and less hard
work. Only occasionally does he write lines of such a
genial and friendly humour as those in *What You Will*
which describe the indifference of a scholar's dog to his
master's studies:

> *Delight*, my spaniel, slept, whilst I . . .
> Toss'd o'er the dunces, pored on the old print
> Of titled words, and still my spaniel slept.
> Whilst I wasted lamp-oil, bated my flesh,
> Shrunk up my veins, and still my spaniel slept . . .
> I thought, quoted, read, observ'd and pried,
> Stuffed noting books, and still my spaniel slept.
> At length he waked and yawned, and by yon sky,
> For aught I know he knew as much as I.

The Lincolnshire man, Heywood, brought northern
breezes to the London stage. Country junketings and
country details save even so evident a pot-boiler as his
Lancashire Witches from banality, and in *A Woman Killed
with Kindness*, that interesting early example of the domestic problem play, they give a thickness and solidity to the
background which suggests a Dutch genre piece turned
into drama.

The melancholy Ford, the only outstanding dramatist
of the Caroline epoch, is remarkable for his bookish
exploitation of ideas taken from Burton's *Anatomy of*

Melancholy, and for a gloomy fatalism which sees men and women as victims of fate. His poetry frequently achieves a soft descriptive sweetness, a melodiousness oddly at variance with the subjects he chose to handle. *'Tis Pity She's a Whore*, his greatest play, reveals this dualism at its strangest. As star-crossed lovers Annabella and Giovanni are among the most pathetic and attractive in fiction; their youth, their initial innocence, the dewy verse in which they make known their love, approach them more closely to Romeo and Juliet than to any other pair. The verse and indeed the whole treatment is often reminiscent of Shakespeare; Ford almost alone among the other dramatists can touch the stops of love and anguish in the Shakespearian manner. The scene in which Giovanni kills Annabella owes so much to the death scene of Desdemona that it could, evidently, not have been written without the Shakespearian model. But it needed more than a capacity for imitation to achieve the healing tenderness of some of Ford's cadences. Annabella's pitiful 'Unkind, unkind' as her lover, like Desdemona's, kills her on a kiss is one of the great moments of English tragedy. But the crux of the whole play is the incestuous relation between these two young lovers whose tragedy arises from the fact that they are brother and sister. Thus a theme which is often latent in the Jacobean drama finds at last an open expression. The plot was distasteful to nineteenth-century critics, but the incestuous theme is stated with a power and passion that fully justify Ford's choice. What is frequently distasteful by any standard is the crudity of detail. Ford destroys the tragedy of Annabella's death by following it with a scene in which Giovanni displays her still palpitating heart on the point of his dagger.

D

The same peculiar mixture of crudity and tenderness characterizes most of his plays. The only exception is his remarkable historical play *Perkin Warbeck*, a beautiful study of a self-deceived man whose character grows to the grandeur of the kingly part he has assumed. In this play, unaccountably neglected by modern producers, there is scarcely a false note.

By the time Ford wrote, in the fourth decade of the century, there was no slackening in the rate at which plays were being written, but a certain decay of vigour had already set in. Meanwhile a class of amateur playwrights had grown up; courtiers, university wits, and Inns of Court men found that the demand for new plays was such that pretty well anything had a chance of being acted. It became fashionable to write a play or so. Almost every poet of repute—Suckling, Cartwright, Lovelace, Davenant—ran off a comedy or a tragedy or one or two of each. The 'prentice hands of the young sparks scribbled amain—

> Pumping themselves for one term's noise so dry,
> As if they made their wills in poetry.
> And such spruce compositions press the stage,
> When men transcribe themselves and not the age.

So Cartwright, himself the most professional of the university amateurs, made mock of the smaller fry.

King Charles I was an enthusiastic patron of the drama. Although the fashion for bringing the players into the palace still prevailed and the Royal Box at the theatre itself belonged to the future, Court taste was already strongly influencing the stage for the last prolific decade before the theatres were closed by Ordinance of Parliament in the autumn of 1642.

It is this period which makes the solid link between Jacobean and Restoration drama, and the fashion set by the virtuous Charles I is the immediate precursor of that maintained by the less virtuous Charles II. This period begins with the still strongly Jacobean Massinger as the greatest figure in the theatre, but ends under the enveloping shadow of James Shirley, expert alike in tragedy, comedy, and masque, supported on the one hand by Richard Brome as a master of comedy and on the other by the now forgotten Lodowick Carlell as the most fashionable of the serious playwrights. Ford, although his great plays are all of this time, never received the recognition from Court or public that was his due.

The characteristic of comedy was rapidly becoming a slick, witty dialogue. Lip service was still carefully paid to the virtues, but the plots were becoming steadily more raffish both in incident and outline and the 'fast' man or woman (hurriedly reformed in the fifth act) was already the popular central figure. Moreover, playwrights tended to set their comedies in London for choice and to give them a recognizable setting and a topical theme. Thus, Shirley wrote *Hide Park* to celebrate the opening of that public pleasure-ground in 1632; the thin story is sustained by good dialogue but the real attraction was evidently the presentation of a foot-racing incident and of a betting crowd at a horse race in the new park. Shackerly Marmion's tedious *Holland's Leaguer* is a shapeless farce supposed to be taking place in the best-known brothel in Blackfriars, which was called by that name. Shirley's *The Ball*, Cartwright's *The Ordinary*, and Brome's *Sparagus Garden* all take London pleasure resorts and topical subjects for their theme. There were exceptions, of course. Heywood was still writing on country subjects, although the theme of his late play, *The Lancashire Witches*, was strongly topical, as it was based on the famous trial of 1633. A prettier exception is Richard Brome's delightful *Jovial Crew*. Brome had been Jonson's servant before he turned playwright and he imitated his methods with a pleasing facility. But the *Jovial Crew* with its Dekker-ish flavour of vagabondage and carefully studied language has a gaiety and charm which recall the springtime of the English drama, although it was produced within a few months of the outbreak of the Civil War.

The more serious and poetical plays, on the other hand, now followed a very long way after the Shakespeare of *The Tempest*. Fletcher's *Faithful Shepherdess*, which had failed in 1609, was revived with applause in the thirties. There were other less worthy pastoral successes. Lodowick Carlell's *Deserving Favourite* with its idealized tribute to the King's dead friend, Buckingham, much pleased the Court. Shirley dramatized Sidney's *Arcadia*. These insipid works point forward to the occasional prettiness of Restoration pastoral, just as the smart worldliness of the comedies foretells the cynicism of the coming epoch.

The interest of the Court was responsible, too, for an increased interest in production and spectacle. The masques of the 1630s with their elaborate mechanism evidently outshone the lesser scenic opportunities offered by the theatre. Shirley's stage directions for the most expensive of all the masques, *The Triumph of Peace*, presented to the King by the Inns of Court at a cost of £20,000, indicate an astonishing elaboration of mechanism. The scene is changed repeatedly; lights are lowered and raised; clouds bearing chariots with enthroned gods and goddesses melt and form, descend and ascend. Even if the achievement came jerking far behind the conception, the mechanism needed would be various and complicated. The old playhouses could hardly create the optical illusions to which the masque was accustoming the eyes of the wealthy. The long closing of the theatres during the Civil War made it possible for the managers of the future to reconsider the question of presentation in the light of the Court fashions of the first Caroline epoch, and the old theatres were doomed for technical reasons before the Puritans closed them.

CHAPTER IV

THE JACOBEAN AGE: POETRY

THE POETRY of the Jacobean Age seems at first only to continue the lyrical and confident splendours of the Elizabethan; the same population of writers covers the first decade of the century. Indeed, far into the seventeenth century and beyond, the huge and precious quarry of Spenser's works still supplied much of the ore for lesser men. Even when the influence of his style had faded, his phrases remained the common property of literature.

Yet before King James was dead, Michael Drayton, an Elizabethan veteran, angrily prefaced his monumental *Poly-Olbion* with an attack on the new poets. 'Verses', he wrote, 'are wholly deduced to chambers, and nothing esteemed in this lunatic age, but what is kept in cabinets and must pass only by transcription.' He was, like most angry writers who fall behind the times, exaggerating the peculiarities of his juniors. Yet verse as it developed in the next two generations became a matter of delicacy and conceit, following, among classical models, Catullus, Horace, and Anacreon in preference to the solid, slower movement of Tasso's epic style or the highly wrought perfection of Petrarch. Petrarch as a model had dominated English love poetry since the days of Wyatt and Surrey. Tasso's influence came in with Spenser, and when Fairfax published his careful and accomplished English translation in 1600 Tasso's sun had already, as far as England was concerned, passed its meridian.

The veterans and the conservatives, since the conservatives were not all veterans, carried on the Petrarchan tradition until it exhausted itself, and were doomed, most of them, to the disillusion which attends those who outlive a fashion. Popular esteem has never quite given back to them what is their due. Drayton, a solid craftsman in several different manners—Petrarchan, Spenserian, or ballad—and a simple, unquestioning patriot, felt for the rising generation the bitterness that the hardworking conventional writer commonly feels for fashionable innovators. *Poly-Olbion*, his greatest work, which embodies a lifetime of reading and observation, is neglected except by the scholar; yet this colossal description of England, county by county, with all the worthies, heroes, and legends of each, is full of apt evocative phrases.

Historic events were Drayton's favourite topics; his choices were idiosyncratic and it is perhaps not surprising that since his time comparatively few readers have been tempted to cut their way through the Cantos of *The Legend of Great Cromwell* or *The tragical legend of Robert Duke of Normandy*. But he was evidently read with advantage by Dryden, which is a just claim to respect. Learned, conscientious, and from time to time finely descriptive, Drayton fails through a certain dryness of imagination; the long-winded poet who stumps resolutely on but never takes wings soon becomes a bore. His most popular works to-day are the short poems, largely adapted from French originals, addressed to his lady under the name of Idea. Here, more than once, as in the famous 'Since there's no help, come let us kiss and part', he achieves a high perfection.

Sir Philip Sidney's long-surviving friend, Fulke Greville, Lord Brooke, is a veteran whose merit is more difficult to define. He was forty-six by the turn of the century, but he lived until 1628 and his works were mostly published after his death. It is difficult to say when most of them were written. His best known prose work is the life of Sidney published in 1652; it is historically valuable but is not, as prose, at all remarkable. His poetry, which varies from the songs and love-poems of *Caelica* to philosophic and political discussions of interminable length and to dignified blank-verse dramas, is the work of a scholar without humour and without much human understanding, but not without feeling. Greville's feeling is that of the retired and discriminating aristocrat, not of the good fellow who frequents taverns. The weary questioning of the sensitive and lonely heart is thoughtfully compressed into the famous chorus from *Mustapha*:

> Oh wearisome condition of humanity!
> Born under one law, to another bound:
> Vainly begot and yet forbidden vanity,
> Created sick, commanded to be sound. . . .

There are moments, too, especially in *Caelica*, of an unexpected rural sweetness, words which half lift the veil on some younger and blither Fulke Greville whom the weight of years and learning had buried:

> I, that on Sunday at the church-stile found
> A garland sweet, with true-love-knots in flowers,
> Which I to wear about mine arms was bound,
> That each of us might know that all was ours . . .

Chapman, the undaunted translator of Homer, belonged to another world, that of the professional writers. Prolific and persevering, he was playwright and poet as well as translator. As an original poet his merit is irregular; as a translator he is outstanding. The opening years of the century saw both his *Iliad* and his *Odyssey*, completed sometimes overfast, but not without much collation of sources and concentrated, intensive study. Until Pope polished up the rugged epic of Greece's heroic age into a form that suited the drawing-room, Chapman had been its principal interpreter for the English. For thousands, besides Keats who paid him a deserved tribute, Chapman has been the channel through which Homer reached them. The translation is not scrupulously accurate and is often heavy-going. At times he introduces moral sentiments of his own, at times expands without authority from his original, and at times mistranslates. Yet it retains, as no other English translation does, the weight and the insistent forward thrust of the original. Keats selected the right simile when he compared the reading of this work to the seeing of a wide landscape ; it is an uphill struggle but the view is worth the climb.

Among the poets of the older school Giles and Phineas Fletcher rank high. The brothers were about twenty when King James came to the throne; although their published work belongs wholly to King James's reign, Spenser is their influencing genius, and the style of their major poems is that of the High Renaissance deriving through Spenser from Tasso and Ariosto. Phineas Fletcher's classical poem, *Venus and Anchises*, written about 1620, is in the same sensuous Italian vein as Shakespeare's *Rape of Lucrece*, with which it can be compared without suffering total eclipse. The heightened catalogue of female attributes in the verses which describe the sleeping Venus as Anchises finds her, have the same

unashamed rich beauty as the parallel description of the
sleeping Lucrece in the earlier poem and doubtless owe
much to it. The bower in which he finds her is Spenserian, but lovely in its own right as well:

> So far in this sweet labyrinth he strayed
> That now he views the garden of delight,
> Whose breast in thousand painted flowers arrayed
> With divers joy captiv'd the wandering sight.
> But soon the eyes yielded the ears their right,
>   For such strange harmony he seem'd to hear
>   That all his senses flocked into his ear
> And every faculty wished to be seated there.

Phineas Fletcher's art is too frankly derivative to place
him among the great, yet he had an imagination that
was fired by great subjects and he could achieve in the
Spenserian manner an assured and impressive style. His
Purple Island, an allegory of the human body, has magnificent if also highly ridiculous passages. The smouldering
evil majesty of Milton's Satan holding court in Hell is
unparalleled; but Phineas Fletcher's Satan, enthroned
fifty years before, in *The Apollyonists*, had evidently been
studied by Milton.

> The mids't but lowest—in Hell's heraldry
> The deepest is the highest room—in state
> Sat lordly Lucifer; his fiery eye
> Much swol'n with pride, but more with rage and hate,
> As censor, muster'd all his company;
> Who round about with awful silence sate.
> This do, this let rebellious spirits gain,
> Change God for Satan, Heaven's for Hell's sov'reign:
> O let him serve in Hell who scorns in Heaven to reign!

If Phineas Fletcher is never of the greatest, he is often
beautiful and always technically good. That is, perhaps,

his fault; he was too quiet and too careful, working away at his rectory in Norfolk and risking no Icarus flights into the experimental and unknown. Fashion has moreover dealt very cruelly with his choice of subject, with the anatomical cantos of *The Purple Island* for instance.

His younger brother Giles, has both greater heights and greater depths. He is unfortunate in the metaphor in which he describes how faithful Christians

Anchor their fleshly ships fast in His Wounded Side.

His subject was *Christ's Victorie* and the first version of the poem appeared in 1610. This work, too, was written in the country and the spontaneous rural passages share the matchless green beauty of the Spenserian landscape:

> The early sun came lively dancing out,
> And the brag lambs ran wantoning about.

The morning light dapples the meadows and the lines gambol with the lambs. All the more effective when they come are the heavy-vowelled, slow-moving verses on the Crucifixion:

The sadded air hung all in cheerless black,
Through which the gentle winds soft sighing flew,
And Jordan into such huge sorrow brake,
(As if his holy stream no measure knew,)
That all his narrow banks he overthrew;
The trembling earth with horror inly shook,
And stubborn stones, such grief unused to brook,
Did burst, and ghosts awaking from their graves 'gan
    look.

Milton confined himself in *Paradise Regained* to the Temptation alone, but he had clearly studied Giles

Fletcher and adopted from him one of his happiest devices, the emphasis on the physical atmosphere, now spring-like, now clouded, now stormy. If Milton's titanic storm and the sudden bright stillness of the dawn owe none of their words to Giles Fletcher, the idea was his; the brag lambs had a great poetic progeny. The interest and the glory of the Fletchers—no small glory either— is to provide the link between the two greatest epic poets of the English language. It is in their work that the gigantic and dissimilar geniuses of Spenser and Milton are brought, for a moment, edge to edge.

Another of the Spenserians who influenced Milton was William Browne of Tavistock, who in *Britannia's Pastorals* fitted a Spenserian vocabulary and imagery into a variety of metres including the rhymed couplet which was to have so great a future in England. His verse is easy on the ear, not very memorable, prettily monotonous at times, but with a limpid water-colour touch when he writes of his native landscape which can be exquisite.

Less ambitious, although no less concerned about the craft of poetry were the lyric writers of these years. Joshua Sylvester, the entertaining translator of du Bartas, wrote, like Drayton, sonnets in the French manner to his lady; he ventures, however, on those quaint, well-observed, concrete similes which were to become, and remain, characteristic of later English verse and prose. His woods in winter, for instance, are 'peri-wigged with snow'. Samuel Daniel's sonnet sequence to his Delia is better known; but neither he nor Sylvester equals in the short love poem the transcendent Campion.

These writers are Elizabethan in feeling, although much of their work belongs to the Jacobean age. They exploited, as all English lyric poets since Wyatt had done,

the Petrarchan sonnet and the courtly attitude to a tradi-
tionally cold lady. They obeyed carefully the rules of
foreign masters, Tasso and Desportes. They studied the
regulation tropes and similes commended in Italian
works on rhetoric so that lines which seem to us full of
peculiar and original meaning may be merely the English
rendering of a stock Italian phrase. Yet, when all these
disillusioning allowances are made, all of them could on
occasion imbue their love-sonnets and pastorals with an
unmistakable personal force, and wield their own language with precision and skill. Campion makes deliberate
use of the simplest phrases and rhymes. His

> Jack and Joan they think no ill
> But loving live, and merry still

has the comfortable jog-trot of the popular song,
although its ingenious ingenuousness is as carefully
wrought as are any of his classical or Italian adaptations.
Campion had, too, a rare but deeply moving religious
vein which links him with the poets of the next generation and more especially with George Herbert.

His experiments with metre [1] were subdued to an
exceptionally sensitive ear; the unfailing accuracy of his
judgement on the sound and stress of words give him a
place by himself among the poets of this period. Others
exceed him in imaginative range, in vigour and colour
and daring, in brilliant felicity of phrase, but few poets
in the English language have been able, by the mere
placing of words, to do so much with so little. He wrote,
like many other poets of the time, so that he might be
set to music, working often in collaboration with his com-
poser, or composing the 'ayres' himself. The subtle mar-

[1] See p. 7.

riage of sounds at which he aimed is lost to us because few ears to-day are sympathetically attuned to the instrumental music of the early seventeenth century. But the limpid and uncomplicated poetry of the words survives all the more perfectly, perhaps, because it was conceived not to be supported by, but itself to support and enrich, the accompanying notes.

Among the poets in the Petrarchan manner, the Scot, Sir Robert Aytoun, does not perhaps rank very high. But he is interesting as the moving-spirit of a group called the Scoto-Britons. It was the darling hope of James VI when he became King of England that the two nations should become as one, bearing the regional names of South and North Britain only, and forgetting England and Scotland in the all-embracing nation of Great Britain. Neither people paid much attention to this, but a group of Scottish intellectuals sought to bring it about, in literature at least, by the deliberate abandonment of the native manner in poetry and, to some extent, in prose. The fashion by which the educated Scot wrote in educated English was thus set for the century. Even so ardent a Scottish patriot as Montrose wrote his occasional poems in the current English manner, and William Drummond, the most distinguished Scottish poet of the century, is a Petrarchan, using a highly cultured English vocabulary. Sir Robert Aytoun, Sir William Alexander, and one or two other Scottish poets came to Court and thus were to a great extent divorced from their native land. The King, who encouraged their Scoto-British intellectual ventures, was not always the kindest of critics. He wrote disparagingly of poor Sir William Alexander's 'hard, harsh, trotting, tumbling vein'.

Drummond was more faithful to his home and preferred, after visiting King James's Court and travelling abroad, to live on his inherited estate of Hawthornden. Writing in the Petrarchan strain he continued, a lonely Elizabethan, a lonely royalist, and a lonely poet until his death at the height of the Covenanters' triumph in 1649. He was a natural solitary, happy—as long as the times would let him be happy—in his pleasant house near Edinburgh with his library for company and the gentle Esk to soothe his thoughts. His poetry is the poetry of a highly cultured gentleman, but he worked at it with a zeal which amounted to passion, and there seems at times to lurk under the carefully wrought effects the pain of a man who longed to be a greater poet than he was, a poet who knew and suffered under his own limitations. Perhaps that is only a kinder way of saying that his verses smell 'too much of the schools', which was what Ben Jonson bluntly told him.

Drummond's fame rests in part on that celebrated visit from Jonson and the conversations which he recorded, although they are hardly conversations since they consist almost wholly of Jonson's obstreperous monologue. Jonson does not come out of it well; he is overbearing, unpleasantly knowing about all his contemporaries, full of scandal, envy, and all unkindness. One sees, with a dreadful clarity, the great man's stature dwindling before the eyes of his discriminating host.

Alone once more—and oh, the sweet silence that falls on Hawthornden as Jonson blusters off—Drummond continued his solitary struggle after greatness. He loaded his verses with all the ornaments of a cultured vocabulary and with phrases despoiled from five languages and fifty poets. Sidney, Ronsard, du Bellay, Petrarch, Spenser, Tasso, and Desportes, all are brought in to midwife this muse in travail. He lacked the one thing that almost all his English compeers had—a natural touch.

Yet this most overwrought, most elaborate of poets has phrases which grapple the mind, like 'the black map of all my woe'; he has passages of a brocaded beauty when the exalted mood is on him and the borrowed treasures of his brain for a moment flow freely:

> Bright portals of the sky,
> Embossed with sparkling stars,
> Doors of eternity,
> With diamantine bars,
> Your arras rich up-hold,
> Loose all your bolts and springs
> Ope wide your leaves of gold;
> That in your roofs may come the King of kings.
> Scarf'd in a rosy cloud,
> He doth ascend the air,
> Straight doth the moon him shroud
> With her resplendent hair. . . .

Although Drummond's southern-looking talent was hardly suited to the Scottish landscape, he had an eye for scenery and could describe it. (He praised the beauties of the 'Lowmond Lake' to Jonson.) That 'scarf'd in a rosy cloud' is prettily observed from the windy skies of his home; and for the cosy voluptuousness of summer woods among the Lothian slopes his phrase 'the hills empampered stand' is surely perfect.

While the older tradition of Spenser and Petrarch continued with apparent vigour, the forces of revolt and reaction were at work. John Donne, that strange compost of medieval sophistry and original conceit, was already influencing some of the younger poets, although the far-reaching effect of his outlook and manner belongs properly to the next chapter. It is enough to say here

that he had scandalized the Petrarchans and made way
for a new kind of love poetry with his fiercely rebellious
attitude to the passions. Poems like his

> I am two fools I know,
> For loving and for saying so
> In whining poetry . . .

generated a thousand of the 'devil-take her' 'What-care-
I' 'Out-upon-it-I-have-loved' variety, profoundly shock-
ing both in manner and sentiment to more traditional
writers.

The change from one fashion to the other was neither
immediate nor total; up to the eve of the Civil War
there were poets who continued the sweet, mannered
Italian fashion, attenuated in such writers as Carew and
Fanshawe to mere arabesques of prettiness, yet saved
from banality by a certain freshness of touch, a certain
aristocracy of style.

It is the crude and massive figure of Ben Jonson, however, that, at the height of the Jacobean Age, overtops
the literary life of the country; and Ben Jonson with his
introspection and self-conceit, his greed for life, his bulg-
ing pack-load of talents, his uncritical mixture of the
greatest coarseness with the greatest sensibility, is a
typically Jacobean figure. He dominated because he
was the outsize reflection of so many of his contemporaries—their enlarging mirror.

He belongs in feeling to this time of break-up and
break-down, when the Court was suddenly full of adven-
turers, when the black and white and silver, with an
occasional olive-green, that had been the predominating
colours of Elizabethan fashion, gave way to *braggadocio*
scarlets and yellows and blues like an apprentice's May-

E

day or a Morris-dance. It was the time when citizens' wives would be ladies and the dubious morals of the Court were reflected in the vices and disorders of an over-spilling capital; when public theatres flourished, actors mingled with gentlemen, and aristocratic amateurs were dancing and masquing for their private pleasures. London, the cauldron of literary life, seethed and bubbled; masques at Court, plays at the Inns of Court. entertainments on every excuse and for all occasions; 'Characters' and poems passing in manuscript from hand to hand; the bookshops in Paul's Churchyard packed with the newest publications; actor-managers clamouring for plays and the public pelting or applauding the result; the young *literati* arguing in the taverns; and in the centre of it all, lord of misrule, author-in-chief, with his finger in every pie, huge, loud-mouthed, bragging Ben.

His career was extraordinary, his output enormous, his influence, during his life, almost irresistible. He collected the younger writers round him, calling them his 'sons', and after he was dead there were dozens more who claimed to have been among them on the strength, perhaps, of having one evening paid for his drinks at the 'Sun, the Dog, the Triple Tun', or whatever was his tavern of the moment.

The contradictions in Jonson's achievement are explained by the contradictions in his life. A man of mean birth and broken schooling, a rolling stone, a bricklayer, a mercenary soldier, he had picked up a vast irregular education by reading everything on which he could lay hands. An indefinite number of alternating characters flourished together in Jonson: the satirical observer of manners who created the whole Bruegel-like gallery of living grotesques in *Volpone*, *The Alchemist*, *The Silent Woman*, as well as in the London junketings of *Bartholomew Fair*, *Every Man in His Humour*, and *Eastward Ho!* Then there is the learned classical scholar who wedged impressive blank-verse translations of Cicero and Suetonius into his tragedies of *Sejanus* and *Catiline*; the literary quarreller who composed the interminable argumentation of *The Poetaster*, *Every Man out of His Humour*, and *Cynthia's Revels*; the carefully conscious writer who collected and considered all that interested him on the subject of his art in the collection called *Discoveries*; the brilliant talker, the knowing and envious scandalmonger; the fastidious and richly endowed poet of many an exquisite lyric and much magnificent blank verse.

An overwhelming personality, he attributed to himself more than he deserved. He believed, for instance, that he had perfected the Comedy of Humours, a form in which each character displayed a certain quality, and, intent on classical rules, he allowed too little credit to the old Morality plays from which the Humours evidently derived. Setting aside his claims as an originator of a style, what stupendous plays they are; the figures—characters, humours or whatever they may be—bounce about the stage twice as large as life, astonishing and delighting the spectator with their acts, and ravishing ears with a hurricane of language. Jonson can give with equal intensity the devotion of the miser :

Good morning to the day; and next, my gold!
Open the shrine that I may see my saint.
Hail the world's soul, and mine! more glad than is
The teeming earth to see the long'd for sun
Peep through the horns of the Celestial Ram,
Am I, to view thy splendour darkening his;

That, lying here amongst my other hoards,
Shew'st like a flame by night, or like the day
Struck out of chaos, when all darkness fled
Unto the centre. O thou son of Sol,
But brighter than thy father, let me kiss
With adoration, thee, and every relic
Of sacred treasure in this blessed room.

or the vision of the voluptuary:

My meat shall all come in, in Indian shells,
Dishes of agate set in gold, and studded
With emeralds, sapphires, hyacinths, and rubies.
The tongues of carps, dormice, and camels heels,
Boiled in the spirit of sol, and dissolved pearl,
Apicius' diet, gainst the epilipsy:
And I will eat these broths with spoons of amber,
Headed with diamond and carbuncle.
My foot-boy shall eat pheasants, calver'd salmons,
Knots, godwits, lampreys: I myself will have
The beards of barbels served, instead of salads . . .

His brawling women clatter:

ALICE: A mischief on you, they are such as you that
take our trade from us, with your tuft-taffeta
haunches. The poor common whores can
have no traffic for the privy rich ones; your
caps and hoods of velvet call away our
customers . . .
URSULA: Peace, you foul ramping jade, you.
ALICE: Thou sow of Smithfield!
URSULA: Thou tripe of Turnbull!

With no less verisimilitude, in a different kind of quarrel,
he can render into faultless verse Cicero's famous
denunciation of Catiline:

Dost thou not blush, pernicious Catiline,
Or hath the paleness of thy guilt drunk up
Thy blood, and drawn thy veins as dry of that,
As is thy heart of truth, thy breast of virtue?

> Whither at length wilt thou abuse our patience?
> Still shall thy fury mock us! To what licence
> Dares thy unbridled boldness run itself!

It was unfortunate that this vibrating talent was lodged with a humour at once doctrinaire, envious and quarrelsome. There are three great plays—*The Alchemist, Volpone, The Silent Woman*: there are three lesser but still wonderfully lively plays, *Bartholomew Fair, Every Man in His Humour*, and the collaborative *Eastward Ho!* The rest is a mass of partly incomprehensible wreckage—glimmerings of wit and white shafts of beauty spring from *Every Man out of His Humour, The Poetaster*, and *Cynthia's Revels*, but they deal at formidable length with a contemporary literary quarrel which no one, since Jonson's death, has been able to unravel. The two classical plays, *Catiline* and *Sejanus*, are monumental failures: he had not the tragic fire.

Tired of the quarrelsome stage, he devoted himself to the masque, arranging elaborate Court entertainments to be set with all the mechanical ingenuity of Inigo Jones. It was a contemptible form of the dramatist's art: Beaumont put the general view into the mouths of two courtiers in *The Maid's Tragedy*.

> What thinkest thou of the masque? . . .

> As well as masque can be . . . they must commend
> the King, and speak in praise of the assembly; bless
> the bride and bridegroom, in person of some god.
> They are tied to rules of flattery.

Jonson made music enough out of these rules of flattery until he quarrelled with Inigo Jones, wrote a rude poem about him, and refused to be reconciled. Cantankerous, embittered, and full of rage against Court and cliques, he continued to hold forth at the last of the taverns he made famous, the Devil by Temple Bar. Here it was that the Oxford don Cartwright and the little plump clergyman Herrick listened to him as the century lengthened into its fourth decade. Even in his last decline the magnetic personality never lost its drawing power.

He ruled the English literary scene for over twenty years, unchallenged, and when he died in 1637 an influence as great was not felt again until the then infant Dryden reached maturity. It was Jonson who shattered the older foreign moulds in which English verse had formed, not—as Donne was more subtly doing—by a different approach to the subject, but by spilling and pouring into English verse the antique vintages of Greece and Rome until the old mould cracked with the pressure. He left Italy and the Renaissance on one side and dreamed of Catullus, Horace, and Anacreon. *The Poetaster*, where it is not obscurely concerned with modern personalities disguised as Romans, is a masterpiece of historical reconstruction based on the widest classical reading. Here Ben Jonson cast himself as Horace in a society in which he moved on equal terms with Virgil and Ovid and triumphed over his enemies by the serene justice of a civilized Emperor. It was the world of his dreams. These Augustan Latins were to him the source of all poetry, these pagans with their unashamed love of life, their verbal skill, and rich humour, their Epicurean philosophy, their amber-haired mistresses.

It is a little ironical that, of all his gigantic output, the first piece which to-day comes into every mind is one of the slightest and lightest of his songs; but there is also a poetic justice in this popular choice. For Jonson in

'Drink to me only' has miraculously transformed one of the oldest and simplest of English traditional metres into a classical manner. The metrical stresses underlying this evocative melody of sound are nothing more recondite than the hopping interchange of the eight syllable line and the six syllable line of popular ballad metre. He did something of the same kind to English poetry, enfranchising the coming generation from French and Italian leading-strings and making them free at once of their own language and the classical world. If it was Donne who affected the shape and nature of their ideas, it needed Jonson's robust personality to throw down for future English poets the restrictive barriers of Italian rhetoric, to set them to take their models where they chose, and to put their trust in the natural qualities of their own melodious and voluble tongue.

CHAPTER V

JOHN DONNE AND CAROLINE POETRY

JOHN DONNE had been one of the best known of the younger wits (the word was just coming into use) who had frequented the taverns of the Strand in the closing years of Elizabeth's reign. Already his strangely worded, resolutely unconventional lyrics were being circulated in manuscript—'Go and catch a falling star', 'So, so break off this last lamenting kiss'. This manuscript habit, which survived throughout the century, created a whole school of clique and private poetry, as well as obscene and satirical poetry, the 'chamber poetry' which aroused the not unjustified wrath of old outmoded Drayton.

The group among which these verses went from hand to hand was not a very large one, but it was gifted enough and influential enough to break down, on Donne's example, the Petrarchan love-lyric. Donne's attitude to love is satirical-sullen; his conventional mistress is a jilt, his conventional lover an angry man bedevilled by an inconvenient infatuation. Some of his most learned critics do not believe that the love-poems refer to actual experience, but Donne's own embarrassment about them after he took orders in later life, rather suggests that they did. There cannot surely be much doubt about the tide of genuine passion which flows in such lines as those from *The Anniversary* which describe a perfected and mutual love:

66

> All other things to their destruction draw,
>   Only our love hath no decay;
> This, no tomorrow hath, nor yesterday,
> Running, it never runs from us away,
> But truly keepes his first, last, everlasting day.

Again, the feeling which inspires that 'Valediction' in which he argues with more fervour than conviction that true lovers cannot be parted in spirit, is unmistakably genuine:

> But we by a love, so much refin'd,
> That ourselves know not what it is,
> Inter-assuréd of the mind,
> Care lesse, eyes, lips, and hands to misse.
> Our two soules therefore, which are one,
> Though I must goe, endure not yet
> A breach, but an expansion,
> Like gold to ayery thinnesse beate.

It seems reasonable to associate poems like these, as well as the lovely *Ecstacy* and at least one other *Valediction*, with Ann More, the young gentlewoman with whom Donne rashly eloped at the age of thirty in 1601. The act was disastrous. His bride was the daughter of the choleric Sir George More, a courtier on the make, who never forgave him. All court positions and social preferments were closed to Donne by this malign influence, and he was compelled with his wife and growing family to live for many years as a poor relation in the house of some of her more sympathetic kinsfolk. A phrase from one of his letters explains the long silences that now overcame his muse: 'I write from the fireside in my parlour, and in the noise of three gamesome children; and by the side of her, whom because I have transplanted into a wretched fortune, I must labour to disguise that from her by all such honest devices, as giving her my company and discourse, therefore I steal from her all the time which I give this letter.'

A man of a tortured integrity, Donne would not seek the security that some of his friends offered him in the Church until he was fully convinced of Anglican doctrine. This did not happen until he was advanced in middle life. His wife died very shortly after. From that time forward he wrote only religious verse and devoted the greater part of his time and talent to the composition of those unique and remarkable sermons which made him, for the last years of his life, the most famous preacher in the country. He died as Dean of St. Paul's, striving to the last that the unregenerate Jack Donne of the erotic poetry might be burnt and purged away.

Yet the pulse of passion still throbs in his devotional verse, with its rich inlay of worldly knowledge and sensation, and its unusually violent exploitation of sensual metaphors (not in themselves unusual) for religious experience. Thus he concludes the great sonnet, beginning 'Batter my heart, three person'd God', with the lines:

> Yet dearely I love you, and would be loved faine,
> But am betroth'd unto your enemie:
> Divorce mee, untie, or breake that knot againe,
> Take mee to you, imprison mee, for I
> Except you enthrall mee, never shall be free,
> Nor ever chast, except you ravish mee.

His Litany, with its wonderfully compact logic, indicates how well he understood the temptations to which knowledge, beauty, and wit expose the highly developed mind Thus he prays God:

> That learning, thine ambassador,
> From thine allegeance wee never tempt,

> That beauty, paradise's flower
> For physicke made, from poyson be exempt,
> That wit, borne apt high good to doe
> By dwelling lazily
> On Nature's nothing, be not nothing too.

Donne was not a particularly original thinker; rather he was a man of a direct and eccentric talent working on a number of inherited ideas—Pythagorean, classical, medieval. 'They say the owl was a baker's daughter'— Donne was absorbed with the metamorphoses of the human body, with the changing aspects of the human spirit, and with the indefinable connexions which link the most disparate objects into a single creation.

Much of his inspiration derived from medieval thought, and there was in his mind the tortuous chop-logic insistence of the schoolmen. But he added to this an introspective determination to pin down a mental state into words, to express the inexpressible in concrete form. Thus in *The Ecstacy* he writes:

> Our hands were firmly cimented
> By a fast balme which thence did spring,
> Our eye-beames twisted and did thred
> Our eyes upon one double string ;
>
> So to entergraft our hands as yet
> Was all the meanes to make us one
> And pictures in our eyes to get
> Was all our propagation. . . .

No English poet earlier than Donne would have turned 'eye-beams' into tangible threads that could first be twisted and then have eyes threaded on them. This is sheer genius expressing the inexpressible. His contemporaries recognized the force of his manner. Those twisted eye-beams were to be stolen by the Petrarchan Thomas Carew and worked incongruously into his light, lush style. There were numberless other plagiarisms and thefts as well as a whole school of imitators.

The marked peculiarities of Donne's writing have caused his reputation to undergo enormous vicissitudes. His influence over the two succeeding generations was paramount. Then he dropped like a stone. By the end of the century he had become an archaic curiosity; Hazlitt in the Romantic age referred kindly to his pretty lines on parting from his mistress but declared that the rest of his work consisted of 'some quaint riddles in verse, which the Sphinx could not unravel'. At the close of the nineteenth century Edmund Gosse drew the attention of literary critics to his neglected beauties and from that time forward his fame has steadily increased. The poet's introspective and uneasy mind is curiously akin to the feelings of the twentieth century. His major preoccupation in his earlier verse was to ensnare the most elusive mental sensations in the net of words—the task which, after all, has been the principal concern of modern psychological novelists since Henry James. His major preoccupation in his later work is to preserve his soul alive from the onslaughts of doubt and death. Both these ambitions arouse sympathetic echoes in the twentieth century.

Donne's popularity will doubtless continue to rise and wane with the mood of the period, although it is unlikely that his remarkable genius will again be forgotten while the English language survives. But peculiarities of style and thought are not always safe models, and it might easily be supposed that those who cultivated Donne's outlook and manner would reproduce only the extravagance and not the greatness of the original. This was not so; for Donne's imitators were many of them sensitive and gifted poets and, moreover, his troubled mind and startling methods of expression truly reflected the uneasiness of the age which was just beginning.

Dryden, at the moment when Donne was dropping fast below the literary horizon, applied the term 'metaphysical' to his kind of poetry. Dr. Johnson took over the word and affixed it rather arbitrarily to a group of whom Cowley and Cleveland were in his view the leading representatives. Later criticism would add Crashaw, Lovelace, Suckling, and a host of others. Since that time the term 'metaphysical' has been a permanent, if unsatisfactory, addition to the terminology of English literature. Dr. Johnson's characterization of their style is, however, succinct and valuable. 'The most heterogeneous ideas are yoked violently together; Nature and art are ransacked for illustrations, comparisons, and allusions; their learning instructs and their subtlety surprises but the reader commonly thinks his improvement dearly bought, and, though he sometimes admires, is seldom pleased.' He concludes with a condemnation based squarely on the eighteenth-century conception of nature: 'Whatever is improper or vicious,' he says, ' is produced by a voluntary deviation from nature in pursuit of something new and strange; the writers fail to give delight by their desire to excite admiration.'

Johnson is right when he accuses both Donne and those who came after him of ransacking nature and art for illustrations; he is right when he accuses them of seeking the new and strange and he is even right when he detects in them the desire to excite amazement. What he does not give them credit for is the humour which relieves and the dexterity which enlivens their most astonishing images, still less for the passionate inner excitement which vibrates through their works.

Insulated by the calm assurance of the eighteenth century, Johnson makes mock of Cleveland's elaborate verses on, for instance, the black sunshine imprisoned in the Newcastle coal mines. But he is mocking unseasonably, for Cleveland himself is not serious; there is an undercurrent of self-mockery, of mock-heroic (or should it be mock-metaphysical?) in nearly all these poets. When Lovelace, describing the battle of Lepanto, marries the sublime to the ridiculous with his 'And the sick sea with turbans night-capp'd was', he expects to raise a smile. Lovelace again has been attacked because, in *Lucasta Weeping*, his mistress, by a fantastic metaphor, has her tears wiped from her cheek by 'the soft hankercher of light'—dried by the sun, in fact; but this is mock-metaphysical again, a deliberate showing-off on his part: 'Look what a quaint conceit I have here.' For those who are deaf to these undertones of self-mockery in the lighter metaphysical poets (Lovelace, Cleveland, and Cowley in particular) much of their verse must necessarily seem offensive and absurd.

By far the greatest of the metaphysical poets after Donne was, unhappily, a man of the utmost gravity. When Crashaw is funny it is not by intent. The mockers have pursued him mercilessly for that misguided comparison of the Magdalen's weeping eyes to

> Two walking baths; two weeping motions;
> Portable and compendious oceans.

It is certainly nothing less than a catastrophe in the work of a man whose heights are among the highest

in the language. The same poem contains the lovely
lines

> The dew no more will weep
> The primrose's pale cheek to deck;
> The dew no more will sleep
> Nuzzled in the lily's neck

—a conceit which is founded in affectionate, accurate
observation and succeeds. Again in his adaptation of a
Latin poem on a singing nightingale he has lines where
the forced juxtapositions and bold metaphors are perfectly mingled with a just observation and controlled
by an exquisitely sensitive ear:

> There might you hear her kindle her soft voice
> In the close murmur of a sparkling noise,
> And lay the groundwork of her hopeful song;
> Still keeping in the forward stream, so long,
> Till a sweet whirlwind, striving to get out,
> Heaves her soft bosom, wanders round about,
> And makes a pretty earthquake in her breast;
> Till the fledged notes at length forsake their nest,
> Fluttering in wanton shoals, and to the sky
> Winged with their own wild echoes, prattling fly.[1]

Crashaw—whose anthological fame for many years
rested on his least typical poem, an address to his
imaginary future wife, 'Whoe'er she be, that not impossible she'—is one of the greatest of our sacred poets.
Born when Donne was just about to take orders, he lived
the quiet life of a scholar until, in the Civil War, his
royalism cost him his Cambridge fellowship. Taking
refuge abroad, he found his final happiness in the

[1] It is interesting to compare Crashaw's treatment with
another adaptation of the same poem in the first Act of
Ford's play *The Lover's Melancholy*.

Roman Catholic Church and died on pilgrimage to Loretto in 1649.

His two hymns to Saint Teresa are well known and cannot be too well known. They combine ecstatic adoration suitable to the great Saint with a wonderful tenderness. The pathos of the lines on Saint Teresa's attempt at seven years old to run away and convert the Moors needs no underlining.

> Yet, though she cannot tell you why,
> She can love, and she can die . . .
> Farewell whatever dear may be—
> Mother's arms or father's knee.
> Farewell house and farewell home
> She's for the Moors and martyrdom.

He moves from this with an absolute control of emotion and measure to the great echoing close:

> O thou undaunted daughter of desires!
> By all thy dower of Lights and Fires;
> By all the eagle in thee, all the dove;
> By all thy lives and deaths of love;
> By thy large draughts of intellectual day,
> And by thy thirst of love more large than they;
> By all thy brim-fill'd bowls of fierce desire
> By thy last morning's draught of liquid fire;
> By the full kingdom of that final kiss
> That seiz'd thy parting soul, and seal'd thee His. . . .

His fault, apart from his uncritical seriousness, was a morbid preoccupation not so much with death (Donne had been absorbed by death and had made poetry of it) as with physical symptoms—blood, tears, sweat. It is strange that a poet who at his best has the incandescent depth of sunset or dawn is, at his worst, rather foetid.

In Crashaw the faults and merits of the metaphysical

poets are most sharply revealed. The poets of the Caroline age do not, however, allow themselves to be severely grouped into schools. 'Metaphysical' is a loose term and so is 'Cavalier'. There are Cavalier poets who are not metaphysical and metaphysical poets who are not Cavalier. It is best, perhaps, to group them roundly by their epoch as Caroline poets, for most of them have a touch of something which, if not distinctively metaphysical or Cavalier, is distinctively Caroline. In almost all, the conflicting influences of Donne and Jonson are mingled in differing proportions.

By the middle of the reign of King James I it had become apparent that great changes were approaching. The tension between Crown and Parliament, between a centralizing and self-conscious King and an intelligent, independent, and ambitious middle class was fast increasing. The hold of the Puritans not only on the middle classes but on every section of society was strengthening. Subtly, and hardly consciously, during the reign of Charles I, poetry itself was thrown on to the defensive. The individual sense of doom in Donne is translated into a general sense of doom among the generation which grew up under James I and began to write under his son. It was not surprising then that they adopted Donne's peculiar outlook almost without knowing it, or fled to the world of classical escapism with its doctrine of present pleasure, offered to them by Ben Jonson.

This second quarter of the seventeenth century was the most prolific in small talents (and some not so small) that the British Isles have perhaps ever known. The reason—if reason can be found for these strange chances—may lie in the coincidence of a period of relative leisure

F

and prosperity among the middle and upper classes with the first maturity of the language as a poetic instrument. Whatever the cause, the effect is certain. Groups of friends and friendly rivals, large and small, devoted their leisure to composing and circulating verses of love and light philosophy, translations and adaptations from the Latin, the Greek, the French, the Italian, and the Spanish. Sometimes they met together, sometimes the circle was maintained by letter. Sometimes it was not an organized circle at all, but a chance association of the tavern or common room. The ladies played their part as the objects of artificial passion under assumed names, or occasionally as poets themselves.

The poets clustered most thickly at the two universities and at Court; Cambridge could claim Abraham Cowley, John Cleveland, Richard Crashaw, John Saltmarsh, Edmund Benlowes, Thomas Randolph, Thomas Pestell, the translator Thomas Stanley, and for a while the young John Milton. Oxford contributed Richard Lovelace, William Cartwright, William Strode, and Jasper Mayne; the Court group Thomas Carew, John Suckling, Richard Fanshawe, William Davenant, Edmund Waller, John Denham, Francis Kynaston, Aurelian Townshend, Sidney Godolphin; the London poets, more closely associated with Blackfriars or the Inns of Court than with Whitehall, number Shackerley Marmion, George Wither, Thomas May, Thomas Jordan. In spite of the ephemeral light-heartedness of their verse, some apparently 'Cavalier' poets were Roundheads when it came to push of pike. These groups, none of which produced any social innovation so definite as the fashionable new French idea, the *salon*, communicated and mutually furnished each other. Representatives of all or any of them might have been found, until his death in 1637, drinking among the 'sons' of Ben Jonson. Robert Herrick, exiled to his regret in a West Country vicarage, made an occasional appearance at Jonson's tavern, or at his old *alma mater*, Cambridge, or at Court where he had once been a chaplain. Flickering in and out among them from foreign travels, foreign wars, and continental exile were such Roman Catholic poets as Patrick Cary and William Habington.

The clergy were partly, though not wholly, prevented by their cloth from a too irresponsible mingling with these erotic, lightly sensual poets. But the writing fever was with them, too, in their studies. Herrick flittered like a moth round the bright light from London. Cartwright and Mayne participated fully in the poetic—and even dramatic—creations of Oxford. Others confined themselves to more strictly religious themes: thus George Herbert and his imitator, Christopher Harvey; thus Henry King, Bishop of Chichester.

Beyond the three chief intellectual centres, over the country far and wide, were gathered smaller and more personal associations. Poetry was not always the subject of their discourse. The house-parties given by Lord Falkland at Great Tew, or Lord Northampton at Compton Wynyates, were more often devoted to the discussion of religion, philosophy, or politics. At Woburn, with the Earl of Bedford, it would be politics and commerce; at Wilton, with the Earl of Pembroke, politics and the chase, with perhaps a little poetry when William Browne of Tavistock was a member of the household; at Bolsover, with the Earl of Newcastle, who turned a stanza himself from time to time, it would be poetry and the chase: it was in this nobleman's protection that James

Shirley placed himself during the war. The easy manners of a peaceful society created these social constellations and, among many, poetry took high place. There was the little group on the Welsh border which included Henry Vaughan and the lady he called *Amoret*, and which was linked with the Cardigan circle of which Katherine Philips ('the matchless Orinda') was for a time the moving spirit. Here and there in remoter places the traces of such groups are to be distinguished. The society of devout Anglicans pursuing their Biblical studies, praying, singing, and story-telling under the leadership of Nicholas Ferrar at Little Gidding, was only a more compact and single-minded group of the kind. Among the private papers of Montrose which aroused the suspicions of his enemies were some letters of fantastic compliment signed with pseudonymous names; for a moment one catches the breath of an Arcadian breeze blowing from the Ochills.

The poetic achievement of these writers was irregular. They have left behind them some of the sweetest lyrics in the language, some of its loveliest religious verse, and also some of its most vapid. They experimented with metres and manners; they helped to develop the rhymed couplet; and they perfected—this was largely the work of Cowley—the English ode. But they also wasted their ingenuity on fantastications: anagrams, riddles, and poems written in symbolic shapes.

The substantial number of names here catalogued, to which many more could be added, indicates the fertility of this astonishing period. Their work—to be savoured by sipping rather than in powerful draughts—abounds in lovely touches, in a sunlit lyricism, shaded with melancholy; in apt or curious or amusing similes; in bold and

startling phrases. They imitate and plagiarize each
other, and their habit of passing poetry from hand to
hand in manuscript has given rise to countless mistaken
or dubious ascriptions. Yet the total effect of their work
is one of liveliness and originality. Their ideas may have
come from a common stock, but the common stock was
new.

There is room here to describe only some of the
brighter luminaries in this milky way of talent. Both
Abraham Cowley and John Suckling very nearly
approach to greatness. Both miss it through some defect
of character, it would seem, rather than of talent. The
precocious Cowley, the cherished son of a merchant's
widow, took to poetry through reading *The Faerie Queen*
which he chanced on at ten years old in his mother's
parlour; by the time he was thirteen he was a poet in
his own right yet he never achieved a complete maturity.
Sensitive and sweet-natured, with a scholar's interest in
technique and zeal for work, he lacked a certain tough-
ness and he lacked ambition. A Royalist, he lost his
Cambridge fellowship and spent many years in exile in
France, circumstances which gradually depressed his
spirits. Full of fantasy and charm, not without humour,
cultured, dowered with an enchanting invention, he
lacks the sinews of genius. His *Elegy on Mr. William
Harvey* contains a touching tribute to that unique
experience of youth, a college friendship:

> Ye fields of Cambridge, our dear Cambridge, say
> Have ye not seen us walking every day?
> Was there a tree about that did not know
> The love betwixt us two?

Yet the whole poem is as far below *Lycidas* as it is above
the usual mourning verses of the time. Cowley is not a

poet whose rather diffused qualities can be conveyed easily in brief quotation. He is a poet whom it is always a real pleasure to read; yet reading him is like walking abroad on one of those mild misty blue days in spring which tantalize continually with the expectation of a sun which never breaks through the clouds.

Sir John Suckling was a very different personality. A courtier and a gallant, he turned off *vers de société* with enviable ease. All his poetry shines with an urban cleverness and some of it is obscene. In his *Session of the Poets* he satirized many of his contemporaries in a manner very useful for literary historians, and with a savage skill. Had he lived to the Restoration he would have been in his element. As it was he sometimes got into trouble and his end was pitiful. Extravagant and a great gambler, he spent what was left of his fortune on equipping troops for the King in the second Bishops' War. His feathered company did not run away any faster than any other section of the army, but having made itself conspicuous it was laughed at a great deal more. In trouble next over the Army Plot, he fled to Paris and died there in 1642, possibly by his own hand, possibly of the pox, and certainly in want.

His neat and careless gaiety has great charm; his cleverness fascinates though his frequent gibes make a jarring note. It is not surprising that this cynical voluptuary was read with approval long after the Restoration; sixty years after his death Congreve's Millamant paces the stage with a volume of his poems in her hand.

He has the distinction of having written one poem which stands quite alone. His *Ballad upon a Wedding* was an early genre piece of a kind that was to be laboriously attempted by many much later poets. It is purely and excellently descriptive, has a touch of the old ballad and just enough of the Suckling spice to give it a flavour. Thus, of the bride:

> No grape that's kindly ripe could be
> So round, so plump, so soft as she,
> Nor half so full of juice.

and of the dinner:

> Just in the nick the cook knocked thrice,
> And all the waiters in a trice
> His summons did obey;
> Each serving man with dish in hand,
> Marched boldly up, like our trained band,
> Presented, and away.

Richard Lovelace, an Oxford man, has rightly gained anthological immortality in a few unmatched lyrics, but his work is irregular. Some of his fame, both living and dead, has, one feels, been due to the beauty of his name and of his person—'a most beautiful gentleman', says Aubrey. He had a genial humour and can be particularly charming about little animals; a grasshopper, a fly, a snail move him to affectionate contemplation. Some have seen in him the most successful imitator of Donne in the use of metaphysical conceits, and he certainly has a compactness, a manner of compressing two or three ideas into a single phrase, which is close to Donne in technique although far behind in feeling.

John Cleveland, of St. John's College, Cambridge, had a mathematically sensitive ear. Nothing else could have carried him safely through the metrical intricacy of his unique

> Never Mark Anthony
> Dallied more wantonly
> With the fair Egyptian Queen.

Like Suckling, too, he had a satiric, topical vein in which, as the political scene darkened, he found a sour relief. The manuscript habit has created some confusion as to the ascription of some of these verses, but the poem on Strafford, circulated anonymously as a broadsheet very soon after his execution, has a smouldering power:

> Here lies wise and valiant dust
> Huddled up twixt fit and just:
> Strafford, who was hurried hence
> 'Twixt treason and convenience.
> The prop and ruin of the State
> The people's violent love and hate.
> One in extremes loved and abhorred.
> Riddles lie here, or in a word,
> Here lies blood, and let it lie
> Speechless still, and never cry.

But he, like Lovelace, indeed like most of these poets, is happiest in his moments of sudden, exact, humorous observation. Thus of a fly on his lady's hand he can write adroitly:

> He tipples palmistry and dines
> On all her fortune-telling lines.

The saintly George Herbert was much indebted to Donne, though his surface simplicity would seem to belie this. A good musician, he wrote many of his poems for singing, and one may trace in him, perhaps alone of later poets, the direct influence of Campion. Herbert's poems clearly reflect his strong and saintly character. Brother of Lord Herbert of Cherbury, the duellist, philosopher, and scientist, and cousin of the Earl of Pembroke, Herbert willingly and without the least ostentation exchanged all the opportunities and pleasures of a courtier's life for that of a country parson, fulfilling his duties to the end of his short life in the small parish of Bemerton near Salisbury. Herbert is one of those perfected personalities that always stand a little apart from the blemished and friable majority of human beings. He was a man of perfectly balanced goodness and his poetry has a serenity which is already beyond passion. For that reason he can never stir the emotions as Crashaw or Donne can stir them; but he can convey the still wonder of unperturbed devotion more truly than any other poet:

> I got me flowers to strew thy way,
> I got me boughs off many a tree:
> But thou wast up by break of day,
> And brought'st thy sweets along with thee.
> Yet though my flowers be lost, they say
> A heart can never come too late;
> Teach it to sing thy praise this day,
> And then this day my life shall date.

A milder religious vein was that of Henry King, Bishop of Chichester, one of the many poets at this time who attempted a metrical version of the Psalms. In his usually competent but rarely distinguished verse the influence of Donne is paramount. In a single poem, the unrivalled *Exequy for his Wife*, he achieves a poignant expression of grief in which his personal manner for once rises superior to the influence of the greater poet whom he copied. There has rarely been anything that quite compares with the patient tenderness of the four lines in which he describes his widowed march towards the longed-for reunion with his love.

> But hark! My pulse like a soft drum
> Beats my approach, tells thee I come;
> And slow howe'er my marches be,
> I shall at last sit down by thee.

Henry Vaughan was a generation younger than Herbert and King. The obscurity surrounding his life has been assiduously (and perhaps unfortunately) dissipated by the patient research of the last fifty years. To-day, the hazy vision of a quiet country doctor penning contemplative poems to his God has been only too vividly replaced by the lively portrait of a litigious and rather dishonest little man who quarrelled continuously with most of his children. Yet it is an interesting story, for something happened to this difficult and rather unsympathetic Welshman shortly before he was thirty. All his best poems were composed within a very few years and all appeared in the volume called *Silex Scintillans*, the sparkling flint, which was published in 1650. What had struck fire from the flint we shall never know; but the fire was worth striking, for it was Vaughan who

> . . . saw Eternity the other night
> Like a great ring of pure and endless light.

It was Vaughan who wrote that lovely sunset lament:

> They are all gone into the world of light

and Vaughan who gives us visions of Heaven innocent and bright as a Fra Angelico painting. It is a comfort perhaps to know that such visions may be had through a Welsh parlour window by a human being no better than the rest of us—except, of course, that he had genius.

The emblematical poets, of whom the two most interesting are Christopher Harvey and Francis Quarles, have an interesting relationship to the metaphysical poets. The fashion of publishing books of woodcut pictures and explanatory verses lasted for nearly a century. The first example is Elizabethan; one of the last is the pretty boudoir-amorousness of Philip Ayres's *Emblemata Amatoria* published long after the Restoration. For at least another two centuries the genre survived among children's books.

These illustrative woodcuts, crude in execution, were extremely bold in conception. Illustrators were prepared to make pictorial images of the most complicated philosophical or theological conceptions. They also made use of a plentiful ready-made vocabulary of symbols, the debris left over from the rich allegorical conceptions of the ages before printing. Thus, winged seraphs balance on globes; sun, moon, stars, and all the figures of the zodiac are personified; gigantic hands issue from clouds to wield compasses or thunderbolts; devils and human beings undergo the strangest metamorphoses or perform the most unlikely actions. These woodcuts did not appear in the emblem books only. They would be scattered about as decorations in many different texts or used on broadsheets. The effect of these popular little pictures, familiar to everyone in their time but unfamiliar to us, was felt outside the narrow sphere of purely emblematic poetry. A good number of the most striking metaphysical conceits—Donne's 'stiff twin compasses', for instance—evidently derived their inspiration from this pictorial source and were sometimes no doubt intended to recall to the reader a symbolic picture with which he would be familiar.

The emblematical poets, proper, are thus closely linked to the metaphysical poets. They were mostly moralists, in a simple, religious vein, and both Harvey and Quarles based their illustrated cycles of religious teaching on Jesuit manuals of devotion. In his strength of phrase now and again Harvey recalls Donne:

> The whole round world is not enough to fill
> The heart's three corners; but it craveth still.
> Only the Trinity, that made it, can
> Suffice the vast-triangled heart of man.

But the echoes from Donne are hollow; he modelled himself more closely on Herbert.

The facile simplicity of the immensely prolific Quarles has a charm which grows with better acquaintance. His fortune at the hands of critics has been a peculiar one. For a hundred and fifty years he was reprinted in cheap editions for the edification of the young, and regarded with contempt by the critics, most of whom did not trouble to read him. 'You will find Quarles's Poems in the lobby,' cries Lady Wishfort to Mrs. Marwood when she wishes to be rid of her for a moment, thus indicating Quarles's position as a safe and colourless author, very suitable for waiting women and companions to read while waiting for their employers. No authoritative recent edition of his work exists, a sufficient indication of his still fustian reputation. Quarles was a simple soul and wrote out of the fullness of a simple heart. The Song of Solomon inspired him to make his Redeemer the object of a gentle lyric love which can be as ingenuously moving as the offerings at a wayside shrine. 'So I my Best-beloved's am: so He is mine', runs one of his prettiest refrains.

But Quarles has had the laugh of the critics in one particular. Whether by a genuine error or through some malicious joke, a poem by Quarles, with only a few minor verbal changes was printed in at least one edition of Rochester's poems. Quarles's odd religious fantasy 'Why dost thou shade thy lovely face?' was thus passed off as a courtly address to a mistress by the prince of

Restoration rakes; as such it appeared in the first edition of *The Oxford Book of English Verse* as well as in lesser anthologies, and in at least one standard History of English Literature Rochester is solemnly commended for these beautiful lines. The work of a poet generally regarded as an honest, virtuous hack was thus successfully passed off, by broad daylight, for the work of an accomplished, aristocratic blackguard. Errors and faulty ascriptions are very frequent in the seventeenth century and this is only the most startling of many; but the long persistence of the error is an eloquent comment on the essentially subjective nature of nearly all criticism.

Among this vocal population of poets, Robert Herrick stood, much against his will, a little apart. Although he counted himself a disciple of Ben Jonson, he was more of an Elizabethan in spirit. His classicism is fresh, innocent, and rather unlearned. He preferred the natural English ballad to any other form. Country pleasures and country legends pleased him, fairies and hobgoblins, fantasies about glow-worms, rhymed charms, and the kind of felicitous doggerel that people carve over mantelpieces and lintels. But the delicacy of his ear, the bold variety of his metres, and the warm glow of his imagery transform his mildest subjects and enliven the most trivial of his quatrains. In a graver mood he wrote some warmly human religious verse, breathing a trustful uncomplicated devotion. He was a little older than most of the Cavalier poets and his career as a country clergyman kept him, except for occasional visits, outside their talkative cliques. He was a buoyant man, well pleased with himself, and when he lost his living for being a Royalist, he hurried up to London, at long last to get his fill of talking to the wits and publishing his poetry.

There were not many wits left by 1648 and they did not see much in his poetry. The rhymed couplet was already sweeping on its triumphant way, and what were the younger men to make of a poet who joyfully exposed to public view such innocent scraps as:

> If ye will with Mab find grace,
> Set each platter in his place;
> Rake the fire up, and get
> Water in, ere sun be set.
> Wash your pails, and cleanse your Dairies;
> Sluts are loathsome to the fairies:
> Sweep your house: Who doth not so,
> Mab will pinch her by the toe.

He had no lofty pretensions but freely admitted his tastes:

> I sing of brooks, of blossoms, birds and bowers,
> Of April, May, of June, and July flowers;
> I sing of maypoles, hock-carts, wassails, wakes,
> Of bridegrooms, brides, and of their bridal cakes.

Herrick was already over fifty, which was old to publish and to be disappointed. He lived another twenty years and died without seeing any recognition of his work. During the whole of the eighteenth century he was wholly forgotten and he had to wait for rediscovery until Maitland's edition of his work in 1823. The recognition, which came so slowly, has been complete, and the natural, rural sweetness of Herrick, his colour, his humour, his limpid music are sure of their place in literature. Sure, too, of their place in memory are Prue, his good-hearted serving-maid, and the 'green-eyed kitling' that played on his hearth, both of whom he was as willing to take into his verse as the imaginary Dianemes and Antheas to whom he addressed his love lyrics.

His particular talent, which could so well express the transient sweetness of a summer frolic or the crackling warmth of a winter festival, may speak an *envoi* to the whole bright gathering of writers who were travelling so fast, with their country, into the bleak season of civil war. Of them, as of those blossoms, 'fair pledges of a fruitful tree', which Herrick saw falling in the wind, he might have written

> What, were ye born to be
> An hour or half's delight;
> And so to bid goodnight?
> Twas pity Nature brought ye forth
> Merely to show your worth,
> And lose you quite.

For many years, indeed, others of these poets as well as Herrick seemed to have bid good night. The fashion was for generations resolutely set against them, and this period, uniquely rich in lyrical talents, was regarded as a mere decadence trailing behind the Elizabethan glory. Its poets remained unedited and unread. It has been the gradual work of the nineteenth and twentieth centuries to restore the Caroline poets and to bring their poems back for something more than 'an hour or half's delight'.

CHAPTER VI

PRACTICAL PROSE

THE PROLONGED, complicated, and often very bitter struggle which filled the middle years of the century affected the life and the outlook of almost every educated man or woman in the country. There may have been a very few whose preoccupation with abstruse studies sheltered them altogether from political and religious controversy and its more violent effects on their lives and minds; but nearly all, however little attracted by nature or fitted by temperament, were involved as combatants or as victims in the painful crisis through which their country was passing.

Politics and war now swept into the universities to deprive scholars of their fellowships and into country parishes to deprive first the Royalist clergy and then the Puritans of their livings. As they sheltered from the blast, some groups of learned men grew closer together. The germ of the Royal Society was in the meetings of scholars and scientists in this sad time.

At Cambridge, and more especially in the Puritan stronghold of Emmanuel College, the group of philosophers known as the Cambridge Platonists continued to pursue truth in the realms of thought. The most interesting and distinguished of them, Henry More, was also a poet. His prose still has the complexity of a language that has not fully found the way to express philosophic

ideas unequivocally, but it has passages of beauty and
the meaning is always worth pursuing. His colleague,
Ralph Cudworth, most of whose work was published
considerably later, had a more powerful if more ponder-
ous intellect, but an unappealing style. The other chief
members of the group were Nathaniel Culverwel, Ben-
jamin Whichcote, and John Smith.

In the atmosphere of angry pamphleteering that now
filled the air, their attempts to establish a sane and
tolerant Christian Platonism stand out impressively.
'There is a perpetual peace and agreement betwixt Truth
and Truth, be they of what nature or kind so ever', wrote
Henry More, after twenty years of bloodshed and mili-
tary government had tormented and divided his countrymen.

The foreshadowed conflict—for every intelligent person had seen something of the kind coming from afar off
—may have intensified the poetic activity of the previous
decades. There was a frantic twittering before the storm
broke. But the new violent conditions worked more
strongly on prose, for prose, whether spoken or written,
public or private, was the foremost weapon of conflict
and nothing sharpens prose like the necessity to do battle
with it. It had, of course, been used in political propaganda before—that could hardly have been avoided; but
all the battling prose of the previous century was hardly
equal to an average year's output during the Civil War.

The most obvious instrument—yet oddly enough the
one that most conspicuously failed—was the sermon.
While the struggle was yet a long way off, the English
sermon had reached its first climax with the staccato
chime of Lancelot Andrewes and the tolling-bell of
Donne. Neither of these belongs to a period of conflict,

neither is a fighting preacher. Their sermons demonstrate facts and beliefs known to all. Although here and there in Donne's great thunders a political note can be detected, he is on the side of an authority which he does not yet feel to be shaken, and his words are the sombre threat of a father who is master in his own house and will tolerate no rebellion in the nursery. He believed, in his own words, in 'the imprinting of persuasibility and obedience in the subject', but he did not envisage a time when that imprinting would be beyond his, or anyone's, power.

His style on this theme is a long way indeed from such a plea as Mark Frank's apologetic defence of the ceremonies of the Church of England in a sermon preached with real courage to a hostile audience of London's puritan aldermen in 1640. Quoting St. Peter on authority, Frank proceeds

> . . . A hat, a knee, a reverent posture of the body, are no such tyrannies as some please to fancy them. You would do more in a great man's presence, more for a small temporal encouragement. A habit, a hood, a cap, a surplice, a name are wonderful things to trouble a devout conscience. You have more ceremonies in your companies and corporations, and you observe them strictly.

When the note of defence, or for that matter the note of attack, comes into the sermon, the whole style alters. The long expository sentences are dissolved into brief colloquialisms; the tone alternates between the exclamatory and the persuasive; lengthy *ex cathedra* judgements are heard no more from the Royalist preachers.

This style, not unnaturally, was now transferred to those in the ascendant, especially the Presbyterians.

It is they who, both in England and in Scotland, insensibly exchange the fighting for the authoritative manner. Thus, from the pulpit of St. Margaret's, Westminster, throughout the Civil War issued the solid platitudes of Stephen Marshall; thus, in Scotland, the wordy Robert Baillie, the pragmatical David Dick, the stalwart Alexander Henderson spoke to audiences of whose approval they were certain.

Eloquence might perhaps be as well displayed by a preacher whether he spoke for a fanatic minority, for the oppressed, or for the Establishment of the day. Yet though there was pulpit thumping of tremendous vehemence, pulpit argument, pulpit persuasion, and even pulpit charm—from such preachers as the Royalist Henry Hammond or Mark Frank—there was very little pulpit eloquence in this tumultuous period. Some sectarian preachers and some of the chaplains in Cromwell's army developed a strong dramatic style new to the pulpit, but the fighting prose of the Civil War came into being on the lips of the men speaking in Parliament and on the scribbling pens of the pamphleteers. It was the men in the front of the battle, soldiers or statesmen, who were tempering English prose to a sharper edge: 'My lords, do we not live by laws and must we be punishable by them ere they be made? . . . Let us not wake those sleeping lions to our own destruction by rattling up a company of records that have lain so many ages by the wall forgotten. . . .' There flashed the sword of an eloquent fighter: it is the King's minister Strafford on trial for his life.

The House of Commons then was a place of short and trenchant speech. The sensible and expressive Table-Talk of John Selden, the leading conversationalist of the legal and Parliamentary world, reveals at its best the crisp and pithy manner of the time:

When you would have a child go to such a place and you find him unwilling, you tell him he shall ride a cock-horse, and then he will go presently: so do those that govern the State deal by men, to work them to their ends; they tell them they shall be advanced to such or such a place, and they will do anything they would have them.

A brisk and vivid English, jewels of an accidental literature, came from the lips of men in action, 'honest brave fellows that make some conscience of what they do'. The description is Cromwell's but it will go for many on both sides. Thus Astley's prayer before the attack at Edgehill: 'O Lord, thou knowest how busy I must be this day. If I forget thee, do not thou forget me', has an eloquent simplicity that fixes it, deservedly, among remembered phrases. So, too, Montrose's persuasively rhythmic words to his vacillating lieutenants: 'Gentlemen, you do your duty; leave the issue to God and the management to me.' So Cromwell's brief comfort to the father of Captain Valentine Walton: 'Sir, God hath taken away your eldest son by a cannon shot. It brake his leg. We were necessitated to have it cut off whereof he died. Sir, you know my own trials this way. . . . There is your precious child full of glory never to know sin or sorrow any more. He was a gallant young man, exceeding gracious. God give you his comfort.' In such phrases as these, and in the pamphlet and the newsletter, a newer, sharper prose was being born.

Milton, as passionately entangled in learning as he was in the coils of his own egoism, learnt little from the new development; he was reserved for a nobler cause.

Here and there in the *Urwald* of his unpunctuated sentences, a vivid creeper hangs glowing: 'I cannot praise a fugitive and cloistered virtue, unexercised and unbreathed, that never sallies out and sees her adversary, but slinks out of the race, where that immortal garland is to be run for, not without dust and heat.' This is poetry that has lost its way, and there is a rhythm which is not quite that of prose even in passages of a more sober colour:

When the Church without temporal support is able to do her great works upon the unforced obedience of men, it argues a divinity about her; but when she thinks to credit and better her spiritual efficacy, and to win herself respect and dread by strutting in the false vizard of worldly authority, it is evident that God is not there, but that her apostolic virtue is departed from her, and hath left her key-cold.

The reasons which have made Milton the best known of the Parliamentarian pamphleteers did not make him at the time the most persuasive or the most popular. He represents less the new, direct manner in English prose than the grand finale of the old, mannered style.

An entirely different type of prose sprang fully armed from the astounding brain of Thomas Hobbes, but it was a kind of prose that was also being evolved at lower levels and in a more stumbling manner by many a practical and scientific writer. Hobbes's *Leviathan*, written during the wars, is a hard, compact, and irreligious elucidation of the political structure as Hobbes saw it. His affiliations were Royalist and the fact that he completed this powerful justification of the right of the strongest to rule in the State at the moment when the King was in exile and Cromwell rising to power was embarrassing to many of his friends. It is not easy to examine the literary merit of *Leviathan* apart from its meaning, a difficulty which is illuminating in itself as it shows how far in Hobbes matter and manner are one. There is no sense of showmanship here, nothing baroque, but a dry, concrete use of English in which meaning and manner are the same thing.

Meanwhile English journalism had come into being, and with it another potent influence on prose style. In the opening years of the century there had been an intermittent supply of occasional bulletins of news called *Corantoes* from abroad. Diplomats and statesmen also employed private men to write them long letters of news from home when they were away. Thus, the letters of the learned and judicious John Chamberlain and later those of the astute gossip George Garrard have been preserved to us among the State Papers and scattered through the correspondence of public men. Not until the outbreak of war did the public demand for news on both sides encourage printers and booksellers to produce regular weekly newsletters. Difficulties of censorship and copyright hampered their early career. Those published in London were constantly changing names, printers, and editors. Only the astonishing *Mercurius Aulicus*, published at Oxford, achieved the record of a regular weekly appearance from December 1642 until the Royalist collapse in the autumn of 1645. The editor, leader-writer, and chief reporter, Sir John Birkenhead, is the true father of English journalism, a lineage of which no one need be ashamed, in spite of Aubrey's rather unkind report of him. ' He was exceedingly bold, confident, witty, not very grateful to his benefactors; would lie damnably. He was of middling stature, great goggly eyes, not of a sweet aspect.' For wit, clarity, compactness, and vigour he has rarely been surpassed. He knew how to present news and how to give it the Royalist slant to suit his readers and himself; he knew how to pick up and respond to the insults of the other party. He never lost a good story by tedious telling, and was adept at turning a scandal into a laugh. 'Rebels brag they took 23 prisoners at Wolvercot Church and were like to have taken the Earl of Dorset with seven of his mistresses together. But his lordship these three months hath not gone forth of the works of Oxford. . . .'

Mercurius Aulicus was the work of a natural born journalist. Other editors were learning; if none can stand comparison throughout with Birkenhead's easy competence, they have good moments, and particularly when returning mockery for mockery they catch a spark of the Royalist humour. Thus *Mercurius Britannicus* from London derides the Oxford *Aulicus* for making up news about 'the taking of some enchanted castle by the Black Prince Rupert, with some dismal conquest over two cottages, and a single buff-coat, or the relieving of a castle with two cows, one calf and ten cheeses'.

The demand for more solid narratives than could be crammed into weekly bulletins of a few small quarto pages led very soon to the publication of special accounts of single battles, or histories of the war over a period of months. Since Parliament controlled the most important centre for printing and publication, the bulk of these appeared under their auspices. Even so, it is surprising how many Cavaliers managed to publish work, often without the printer's name or the place of issue, in the heart of the enemy stronghold. Cavalier or Roundhead, these writers aimed at presenting as clearly as they could,

to a civilian public, exactly what had taken place. Great
literature their works are not, but they introduced a
whole public to a new forthright manner of expression,
they gave English prose a briskness, and sometimes a
brusqueness, that it had not had before. They empha-
sized, as accounts of fighting must emphasize, the little
significant things: in an assault on a country house, the
position of this outhouse, the trees in that orchard; in a
battle, the course of the stream, the slant of the planta-
tion, the slope of the hill. It is the introduction of the
solid topographical detail into narrative, a custom which
once learnt was not easily forgotten. Defoe, and others,
learnt from it.

From these *ad hoc* books about the war it seems but a
step to the set histories; but the step is a large one.
Although party propaganda is naturally pre-eminent in
all these pamphlets and newspapers, their chief purpose
was to give information, more simply to tell a story.
This was rarely the chief intent of the general histories
of the war. Some of them were consciously intended as
works of literature; all of them were intended to serve
political or personal purposes. None, or few, of them
have the immediate freshness of the hot-from-the- printer
current booklets issued while the fighting was in progress.

Clarendon's *History of the Great Rebellion*, one of the
major masterpieces of English historical literature, was
written in part as an instructive manual of politics for
the adolescent Prince of Wales, and in part as an
apologia for the career and conduct of its author. Considering that it is the result of cobbling together two
manuscripts written with different intentions and at widely
separate intervals, the superficial effect of unity in this

great work is truly remarkable. Of its peculiar merits and defects as an historical source it is not here necessary to speak. As a work of literature its position is unchallenged, so unchallenged that surprisingly few people trouble to read it. This is a pity, because the texture of the book cannot be appreciated in extracts. For the sake of easy generalization it has become the fashion to say that the characters are most remarkably drawn. Clarendon certainly took pains over them, but they are of rather irregular merit and much marred by evident personal passion, not to say spite. (Clarendon's judgement of men was, incidentally, as peculiar and as unreliable as that of his royal master.)

Clarendon's style is persuasive, business-like, and clear —a good lawyer's style; but his real genius lies in narrative-exposition. The unobtrusive skill with which he keeps the whole of his crowded story moving smoothly and firmly onwards has rarely been matched. The fact that he sometimes gets his chronology wrong is, for the literary critic, of no importance; for he solves with ease and elegance some of the knottiest problems of narrative history. His sequences are usually clear, always plausible, and always interesting. His opening book on the causes of the war should be a set subject for all postulant historians; it is a model of scene-setting. Every element in the situation, every event, every personality is 'placed' exactly as Clarendon wishes. A first-class legal mind and an educated but unaffected manner have combined to produce a masterpiece in foundation-laying which accounts in great part for the solidity of the whole book and which is worthy of study in itself.

From Clarendon, the drop to any other historian of the war is a long one. Few of them have claims as literature although many are interesting for the unconscious revelation of personality, and nearly all have memorable phrases. The works of Whitelocke and Rushworth are both mere compilations. Thomas May, official Parliamentary apologist, is tedious. Edward Walker, the conscientious chronicler of the King's last two campaigns, is reliable but without literary charm. The two prolific Parliamentary historians, Sprigg and Vicars, hiss and crackle with righteous wrath, but are more rewarding for the student of history than of literature. Perhaps the nearest approach to literature of them all is the contemporary anonymous translation of Wishart's *Gesta Montrosi*. This is a spirited account in good, nervous English of the epic campaigns in Scotland. A rather curious counterblast, Patrick Gordon's *Britane's Distemper*, qualifies for a place in literature. The work, written in something between the King's English and the old Scots-English was conceived as a vindication of the Gordon clan. In its passionate preoccupation with honour and heroism, its romantic magnification of everything to do with the name of Gordon, its lyrical excitement in victory and extravagant anguish in defeat, it is the last spontaneous, anachronistic echo in the English language of heroic literature.

Memoirs and diaries the war produced in great numbers, some men writing because they wished to justify their conduct to the world—thus Edmund Ludlow and Denzil Holles; others because they felt the times to be of historic interest and were determined to record for posterity the events in which they too had played a modest part—thus Philip Warwick; some men, and more women, wrote to rescue from oblivion or disrepute those whom they had admired or loved. Alike in nothing else, the sanctimonious Lucy Hutchinson's valuable life of her dead husband and the fantastic Duchess of Newcastle's intimate account of her living one have this sentiment in common.

The obituary notice had not yet come into being as a literary or journalistic form, though its beginnings can be traced in the journals of the time and perhaps also in the brief lives of the distinguished which became popular reading. Of the various collections of biographies which were now issued, Fuller's *Worthies* is the best known, a warm and entertaining work packed with information. Fuller, a Royalist clergyman, for a time dispossessed, boasted that 'no stationer had ever lost by him'. His output was enormous—history, biography, and moral reflection—all in a pleasant, unaffected, sufficiently graceful style, and with a personal humour, observation, and colour which is at its best very delightful.

John Aubrey, the amiable scatter-brained unfortunate antiquary, who investigated Avebury and made a number of interesting collections on topography, antiquities, and ghosts, is remembered with most gratitude for the great quantity of little personal sketches of his contemporaries and recent predecessors that he left and on which Anthony Wood drew for his *Athenae Oxonienses*. To his insatiable curiosity, minute observation, and alert ear for gossip we owe many an odd and vivid detail of the characteristics of the great. The reader will have found a number of them, and will find more, in the present text.

Among the immense collection of personal writings left from this period of the seventeenth century—letters, diaries, notes, and fragmentary jottings—few are remarkable as works of literature but almost all are valuable as records of personality. In them, even more than in the set histories, occasional vivid, sweet, or touching phrases stand out. Thus, in a scorching phrase, typical of the period, Richard Symonds, a gentleman trooper in the King's Life Guard, blisters the name of a turn-coat: 'Walter Baskervile . . . first for Parliament, then for the King, then theirs, then taken prisoner by us, and with much adoe got his pardon, and now *Pro Rege*, Godwot.' Gervase Holles, excusing himself for writing at great length about the accomplishments of his only child, who had died at the age of three, shoots home a single, parting shaft that the greatest master of pathos might envy: 'I hope I shall be excused for saying so much of this little boy. He was born my heir and this is all his inheritance.'

Through writers like these it is possible to see, clear and minute, as through the wrong end of a telescope, the unimportant moments, the ordinary pleasures, anxieties, and occupations of a world long dead. It would be palpably false to say that all these writers wrote unself-consciously. Many of them wrote with a profound consciousness of self, thinking first and all the time of the impression to be conveyed to the 'unsatisfied'. But they had no burden of already existing personal litera-ture to clog their inspiration; they had not learned the thousand commonplaces and short cuts to emotion that even the most innocent writer to-day will use. Therefore they wrote naturally with a cleanness and a freshness of emotional expression that perhaps not one in twenty of them would have if they were writing now. This—the middle years of the seventeenth century—was the great period for literate amateurs; their language was young and flexible, their vocabulary sufficient and not yet stale.

Their influence on literature was to be considerable.
The emancipation of the *literary* language had been
achieved in the first quarter of the century, when
English poets had learnt to experiment with all its
various, rhythmical qualities and to create for themselves in it an imagery that suited them and was not
merely borrowed from Italian hand-books. The emancipation of what for lack of a better term might be called
the *educated* language took place in the second quarter of
the century. It is a process of great importance in the
evolution of English—or of any—prose.

Until 1640 legal proceedings continued to be reported
—though of course not conducted—in a barely credible
jargon of debased Anglo-Norman French and Latin. A
judge was observed to 'shake son capit', and we find a
prisoner indicted who 'drew his sword sur le stairs' and
another who 'ject un brickbat que narrowly mist'. Until
the middle of the century learned and professional men,
on the whole, preferred to write in Latin. At the beginning of the century most noblemen's households employed a secretary not merely to write, but to *compose*
letters according to the correct formulae. From all this
it is clear that there was a considerable lack of confidence among educated men as to the use of the spoken
language for writing. With the conquest of English for
literature it was evident that the ordinary, educated
man must begin to express himself on paper without
embarrassment, and would in consequence evolve something between the spoken and the literary style for
everyday practical purposes.

The evolution of this style in a hundred different
personal ways can be followed in the Verney Papers, the
letters of Lady Brilliana Harley, the travel memoirs of

Sir William Brereton, the jottings of Richard Symonds, Henry Slingsby, Hugh Cholmley, or—in a different social stratum—of the Lancashire carpenter's son, Adam Martindale; or, north of the border, in the diary of the tormented, neurotic Warriston, or the letters and journals of the warm-hearted minister Robert Baillie. The introspective devout were moved more and more towards describing the process of their lives, God's mercies to them, their conversions, lapses, and doings for the Lord and their fellow men. Richard Baxter's account of his life is vivid reading. But the simplicity of the Quakers lent itself best to this genre. The *Journal* of George Fox stands alone; but Thomas Ellwood's rather naïve and slightly sententious account of his life, with his recollections of Milton, is of considerable interest.

As soon as the ordinary educated man could trust himself to write whatever he chose, he was bound to set himself up as a critic of English prose. Even if the necessity for reporting and the demands of the war had not gone far to break down the old mannered prose, the evolution of informal written English was bound to kill it stone dead. The frontier of a new age has been crossed when a young woman scribbling by the parlour fire can describe a friend and her betrothed with such vivid ease:

'Tis the most troublesome, busy talking little thing that ever was born; his tongue goes like the clack of a mill, but to much less purpose. . . . I admire at her patience and her resolution that can laugh at all his fooleries and love his fortune. . . . Two or three great glistering jewels has bribed her to wink at all his faults, and she hears him as unmoved and unconcerned as if another were to marry him.

It may be argued that Dorothy Osborne, who wrote

these lines, is not a fair example. The letters she wrote to William Temple before they were married were not published until two centuries later in the appendix to a solid life of her husband. It was Macaulay who immediately recognized their value and charm. She was undoubtedly that rare thing, a natural letter-writer. Yet had she lived half a century earlier, not all her spontaneous charm and taste could have helped her to string sentences with such a natural ease.

To this new uninhibited capacity for expression we owe the increasingly numerous day-books, jottings, and personal diaries which mark the middle and latter end of the century. A natural diarist is, on the whole, a more unusual phenomenon than a natural letter-writer, if only because the habit of conscientiously keeping a diary is not normally associated with the characteristics that make for natural and amusing writing. For one good diary there are always a dozen which are merely tedious or self-important. The *Diary* of John Evelyn might well be both these things, for he was extremely self-conscious and inclined to a certain pompousness, but his sense of his own importance was greatly mitigated by his interest in and curiosity about the world in which he lived. His diary thus becomes a record of interesting things seen, experienced, or discussed by him or his circle. It covers more than fifty years. The writing clearly conveys the pleasant, serious personality of Evelyn himself, and throws an interesting light on intellectual society in the last half of the century. If Evelyn rather frequently records disapproval of the morals of Charles II's Court— his description of Louise de Querouaille's interesting collection of *objets d'art* is punctuated with shocked asides on the character of their owner—it is a valuable corrective to the popular view of that Court to remember that the sage Evelyn was *persona grata* there and that the greater number of its frivolous inhabitants shared his more serious interests.

But no other diary of the time, or indeed of any time, can be compared with that of Pepys, in whom the capacity to keep a diary regularly was mingled with a natural gift for good writing. The circumstances are peculiar and possibly unique. This detailed, vivid, and frank diary—which covers nine years—was intended exclusively for his own interest and was written in a shorthand which remained undeciphered until more than a hundred years after his death. It is thought that he noted down the day's events as he went along and wrote up the diary at his leisure, perhaps every two or three nights. Whatever his method, the effect is quite unforced. Even such tremendous descriptive passages as that of the Fire of London do not read like a set-piece, but like a spontaneous account by some admirable *raconteur*.

Pepys does not need a Fire of London to make him interesting. He led a varied and extremely eventful life, working at the Admiralty and in and out of the ante-rooms of the Court. But had he led a life of far less intrinsic interest his Diary would still be absorbing. He can make us follow with sympathy the unattractive marriage negotiations for his despised sister 'Pall' to an inferior husband. His silly wife, with her justified jealousies, her social agitations, and her domestic troubles, is as touching and entertaining as any character in fiction—which is as much as to say, far more entertaining than she can possibly have seemed in the flesh. This observant, alert, social climber, quick and lecherous, with his genuine patriotism, his considerable administrative ability, and his unabashed excitement about life tumbles out on to his pages a whole noisy, lively, variegated, swarming world of men and women. Since the Diary was deciphered (and that is now beyond the memory of the oldest historian) the reign and the Court of Charles II have been seen through the eyes of Pepys. He has truly taken possession of a whole period.

John Evelyn began his Diary when the Civil War was breaking out. Samuel Pepys began his in 1659 when the long period of storm and change was over and King Charles II was soon to be called home. In the interval both subterranean and surface changes had taken place in the thought and style of writers. Much had died, much had been born, or come to a slow maturity. The wars did not make a break in the tradition, although they caused certain distinctive changes. The elements of difference between the world of 1640 and 1660 are at first more obvious than the fundamental elements of sameness.

The strange and solitary figure of Milton spans the gulf.

CHAPTER VII

JOHN MILTON

HAD JOHN MILTON been killed in 1643 'when the assault was intended to the city', the name of this eminent Roundhead would have greatly enriched the list of Cavalier poets. For what are *Comus, L'Allegro, Il Penseroso* but the very height and ecstasy of Cavalier poetry? As the King's personal government drifted to an inglorious close, the Provost of Eton, Henry Wotton, the old courtier, diplomat, critic, and gallant author of 'Ye meaner beauties of the night', read them over and delighted in their beauty.

Milton spans the whole central conflict of the century; he was born in 1608 and died in 1674. In private and in public life he cuts a slightly ridiculous figure, a fact which enhances the solitary tragedy and grandeur of his achievement. That he was humourless and vain cannot be denied; his failings as a husband, a tutor, and a father have been unfairly dwelt on and considerably exaggerated. That his first wife left him after scarcely a month's trial suggests a certain hastiness on both sides; she was a Cavalier and Aubrey neatly expresses the domestic dilemma: 'two opinions do not well on the same bolster'. That he took her back and supported her Royalist relations when the war had ruined them is very much to his credit; that his daughters complained of having to read and write so much for the greatest poet and one of the greatest scholars of his age after he became blind is—if we accept the story—more to their discredit than to his.

What matters here is his career as a poet; and the outstanding thing about that is its self-consistency. With all the political and personal vicissitudes through which he passed, with all the violent storms, the paper quarrels, the veering and backing of his opinions on divorce or the censorship, he remained wonderfully and patiently true to his ideals as a poet. The young man who woke on a showery summer morning to hear the metronomic tap of the rain, the 'minute drops from off the eaves', and to imagine the sober dawn 'kerchief'd in a comely cloud' is in all qualities of poetic observation the same who thirty years later described the rainy dawn in the Galilean wilderness:

> Thus pass'd the night so foul till morning fair
> Came forth with Pilgrim steps in amice grey;
> Who with her radiant finger still'd the roar
> Of thunder, chas'd the clouds, and laid the winds,
> And grisly Spectres, which the Fiend had raised
> To tempt the Son of God with terrors dire.
> And now the sun with more effectual beams
> Had cheer'd the face of Earth, and dried the wet
> From drooping plant, or dropping tree. . . .

The increase in economy, force, and skill, the difference in melody and orchestration between *Il Penseroso* and *Paradise Regained* is remarkable. Did any other poet travel further? Did any other poet travel so far? But the movement is all in the same direction. It is all with absolute fidelity to the same at once sensuous and spiritual inspiration.

Milton, like Shakespeare, cannot be described or explained in the terms of his time alone. The superficial qualities of his early poetry were those of his contemporaries; in many of his personal characteristics he was simply a seventeenth-century Puritan with the failings and the virtues of the type. But that part of his nature which was his genius is outside any generalizations. It would have been possible, had he died young, to regard him merely as the outstanding poet of the group to which his earlier work seems to belong, a richer Cowley, a more powerful Crashaw. The stupendous works of his age make it necessary to reconsider his poetry as a whole; such consideration reveals how far John Milton stands outside the usual development of his time. Starting under the same influences as the other Caroline poets, he did not end where any of their survivors ended, but trod austere heights of his own whither no other English poet has been able to follow.

Milton's natural gifts were an exquisitely sensitive ear; an unusually powerful sensual imagination; a tenacious memory whether for facts, words, physical sensation, or, it must be admitted, other people's poetry; singleness of purpose; and immense powers of concentration. His natural defects were lack of humour and a fundamental lack of interest in ordinary human beings. (That he is far more interested in God, Satan, and the angels than he is in Adam and Eve is a truism; but even in *Comus*, written before he was thirty, he puts his richest treasure of poetic imagery at the disposal of Comus rather than of the Lady and her brothers.)

Milton's acquired qualities were an understanding of several foreign and classical tongues, which enriched his experience in handling metres; a colossal learning which widened his vocabulary and his command of allusion and metaphor; and, at the end, a resigned philosophy of existence.

The traditional separation of Milton's literary life into three sections—early poems; long interval for political writing; late poems—has not helped the understanding of his verse. His poetic development is continuous; during the long war period, which is punctuated only by a dozen sonnets, his belief in poetry as the ultimate end of his life ('that one talent which is death to hide') never faltered. The processes of thought were powerfully at work. He made no false starts on *Paradise Lost*, which he seems to have begun in private during the war. When he had finished his greatest poem he had worked out to the last detail the kind of blank verse in which he wanted to write, the imagery, the vocabulary. To have moved from the flower garden of *Comus* to this majestic mountain-side on the stepping-stones of twelve sonnets would have been impossible. What had gone on in Milton's mind during his silence was a complete generation of poetic development.

And so back to the Cavalier poems which have in them the germ of poetry so much the antithesis of anything that can be called Cavalier. It is easier to explain the development of genius by itself than by reference to outside circumstances, and *Paradise Lost* is more the outcome of *Comus* than it is of the outside circumstances of Milton's life. What distinguishes these early poems from any of their contemporaries is the author's far greater range and easier assimilation of the current influences. There is a little of Donne, rather more of Ben Jonson, a great deal of Renaissance Italy and the classics. There are a sprinkling of metaphysical conceits and a good deal of a young man's showing off. (Those catalogues of gods and goddesses seem to overflow with a kind of exuberance of scholarship from the poet's extensive reading.

Yet he handles names already as easily as Shakespeare: 'Harry the King, Bedford and Exeter, Warwick and Talbot, Salisbury and Gloucester. . . .' 'Peor, and Baalim, Forsake their temples dim, with that twice battered god of Palestine, and moonéd Ashtaroth. . . .')

There is, above all, a complete mastery. Even in his earliest adult and possibly least successful poem, *On the Morning of Christ's Nativity*, he is already ahead of all his contemporaries in controlling the ideas and metaphors that flow into his mind. For a young, relatively unpractised poet on a choppy sea it is astonishing how much sail he can carry.

Although he lacks the sense of individual humanity which gives so touching a sincerity to some of the lightest of Cavalier conceits, there is no mistaking the profound feeling behind these early poems. It has been rightly suggested by Dr. Johnson and others that Milton was not particularly touched by the personal loss of Edward King, the subject of *Lycidas*, in 'that fatal and perfidious bark'; but he was moved profoundly and unmistakably by the ideas which Edward King suggested to him. Cowley's genuine human tears on the coffin of his 'sweet friend Mr. William Harvey' are a trivial passion compared to the surge of angry bereavement, the sense of cosmic loss which inspired *Lycidas*. Again, the little human figures in *Comus* may be nothing but pretty puppets, but the poet's real concern with an idea, with the quality of chastity, is powerful enough in itself to carry the whole drama. Indeed, the closing lines of his masque, written for a nobleman's children, do not seem so much as thirty years away from *Paradise Lost*. Here the poem suddenly and unexpectedly sheds the foliage which has hitherto enveloped it; the last speech of the Guardian

Spirit is as simple a statement as any that Milton was later to make of his fundamental philosophy, his pre-occupation with the relative power of Good and Evil.

Comus, the most significant of Milton's early poems, like *Paradise Lost*, represents a conflict between Good and Evil, the tempter and the tempted, a childish innocence and an age-old cunning. A little girl is lost in a dangerous wood but found again before she has come to harm from robbers or prowling beasts. The young Milton adapts the slight adventure, suitable for a family charade by three children, to a high theme; this time the Lady, lost in the forest, is captured by the evil spirit Comus who tempts her in vain. She refuses the alluring cup and is rescued. Good triumphs over Evil. It was all as simple as that in 1634 when *Comus* was written. Thirty years later, disillusioned by life, only too well aware that Good rarely triumphs over Evil in this world and that lost children are not always found, Milton worked out the same theme in reverse, the theme in which the guileless Eve tastes the fruit the tempter offers. The triumph of Good in *Paradise Regained* was only superimposed later on the original plan which ended with the expulsion from Eden.

The fashion of poetry in the middle years of the century, while Milton's genius was growing in its long incubation, was away from blank verse. With Waller, Denham, and Davenant the heroic couplet was being born. The long narrative poem had never died. There had been Davenant's unreadable *Gondibert*; there had been Shackerley Marmion's enchanting *Cupid and Psyche*, Chamberlayne's *Pharonnida*, Chalkhill's *Thealma and Clearchus*. Cowley, by many still thought to be the out-standing poet of the time, was at work on *Davideis*, an ambitious epic on a sacred theme, ingeniously handled in heroic couplets, with an occasional alexandrine to break the surface. But Milton determined on blank verse.

At the close of *Comus* and in those intervening sonnets, he had stripped his poetry of all superfluous ornament, leaving it no other beauty but that of economy and aptitude of words wedded to a perfectly modulated metre. Now he cast away the last facile adornment left to his muse. He abandoned rhyme. By doing so he lost the chance of popular success, but he was far beyond caring about that. In so far as he still wanted or needed the praise of the judicious, he had it. Marvell approved the poem; the young and transcendently successful Dryden acclaimed it, although he mildly criticized its deviation from classical rules.

The colossal subject of the Fall of Man was popular in the seventeenth century, and not only in English verse. Milton borrowed from the Dutchman Vondel, from the Italian Andreini, and from many others in his epic. Satan and the awful gloom of Hell had inspired some of the finest work of Phineas Fletcher, Crashaw, and Cowley; the theme of *Paradise Regained* had been treated by Giles Fletcher in his beautiful epic *Christ's Victorie.*

The strangely isolated character and the stubborn originality of Milton's genius came out not in his choice of theme but in his treatment of it. The wonderful forward march of *Paradise Lost*, the subtle concealed interplay of natural stress, metre, and meaning which give to the poem a variety like that of the waters of some huge swift river, were evolved in the period which was just deciding that the trim stopped-couplet was the completest form of expression.

With *Samson Agonistes* Milton moved in his solitary

darkness one step farther away from the fashion, this time using a wonderful variety of metres, some rhymed and some not, evolved each one to suit the occasion in the drama or the person who speaks. The uncompromising bareness of diction in *Samson Agonistes* is so successfully built up into a great conception, the simple words and sentences sweep up so naturally into the monumental architecture of the whole poem, that the extreme simplicity of some lines and phrases is startling when they are examined out of context. It may be that in his long darkness the poet was able to turn over recollected visions in his mind's eye and concentrate on their recreation in words with greater intensity than would have been possible had a host of daily visual images been constantly presented to distract his eye. The visual images created by the blind poet of the last poems have an unhindered clarity of focus.

The puritan temperament has certain repellent characteristics—what temperament has not?—and Milton had his full share of its faults. But only on narrow and trivial criteria of judgement can he be denied his place as one of the greatest poets of the world. His themes were the fashionable ones of his period, but they were great themes: sin, death, redemption, and eternity. In him there was also the perpetual preoccupation, which enveloped all others, with Good and Evil. It is implicit in *Lycidas* and the *Ode on the Morning of Christ's Nativity*, hinted at even in the fledged notes of *L'Allegro* and the rippling gravity of *Il Penseroso*, explicit for the first time in *Comus*. As Milton's age drew on he saw the Good in which he believed succumb to the Evil in the world. In his three great final poems the theme of Good and Evil is three times stated and worked out. In *Paradise Lost* the temporary triumph of Evil is established; in *Paradise Regained* the ultimate triumph of Good in its divine form is stated; in *Samson Agonistes* the theme is human and the triumph of Good is won only after defeat and at the cost of life itself. It is unnecessary to labour the parallel between Milton's own life and the theme of *Samson*. This preoccupation and Milton's final solution of it—or resignation to it—has universal value. He is among the few who had something significant to say on an eternal subject and could say it.

The age of King Charles II knew that he was their greatest poet, though his political record and his tastes placed him outside the coffee-house and pleasure-garden centres of their literary life. There was one other poet for whom they felt the same half-guilty respect. This was Cowley. After Milton it seems trivial to drop once more to Cowley, but there is a pathetic parallel here, for Cowley began as Milton did and at about the same time. He, too, was a precocious poet, he too a brilliant young Cambridge man. Time has shown his early lyrics to be thin compared to Milton's but it is understandable that they did not immediately appear so. He, too, like Milton, had a conscience, a Royalist one. He, too, was silent for nearly twenty years while he acted as decoding secretary to the Royalist Court abroad—an interesting parallel to Milton's Latin secretaryship under Cromwell. When he began to write again he wrote a religious epic. *Davideis* has some lovely lines, lovely with the opal hues of the rainbow; yet it is all, somehow, too light and watery for the majestic Biblical subject.

> With richer stuff he bad Heav'ns fabric shine,
> And from him a quick spring of Light divine.

Swell'd up the Sun, from whence his cherishing flame
Fills the whole world, like him from whom it came.
He smooth'd the rough-cast Moon's imperfect mould,
And comb'd her beamy locks with sacred gold . . .

This is a lesser Creation than Milton's:

Let there be light, said God, and forthwith Light
Ethereal, first of things, quintessence pure
Sprang from the Deep, and from her Native East
To journie through the airie gloom began,
Sphear'd in a radiant Cloud. . . .

Cowley was revered by Dryden (surely the most courteous and generous-hearted of successful young men).
When he died in 1667, a disappointed man, he was buried
with the genuine lamentations of the literary world in
Westminster Abbey. Tacitly, his fellows recognized that
here was a great poet *manqué*, but the failure was near
enough to success to be respectable and not ridiculous.
But compare Cowley to Milton and there is, in one single
and close contrast, the difference between parallel talents,
sensibilities, and misfortunes, with and without genius.

Andrew Marvell, the friend and protégé of Milton,
provides a parallel of a different kind. He was of a
younger generation—born in 1621—and since the Civil
War began when he was twenty, he can have cherished
no illusions about life. He did not hasten to write poetry
while the deceptive calm of King Charles's happy years
still reigned. His 'Cavalier' period is therefore, in a sense,
imitative, and although the technical influence of Ben
Jonson is very noticeable, and there are interesting
approximations to such very Cavalier poets as Lovelace
and Carew, the general effect is at once more solid and
more contemplative. The political moral of *The Ber-*

mudas is never far absent from his mind, and in the remarkable *Horatian Ode on Cromwell's Return from Ireland* he achieves an astonishing marriage between the classic elegance of a Cavalier formula and a strong political, half-satirical expression.

Happy for him had he maintained this balance, but the success of his party turned his talent more wholly to official State poetry. There is great technical skill and some beauty, but no saving hint of satire in his poems on Cromwell's later triumphs or on his death. As a poet he had committed himself too far; he could never now, with the collapse of the Puritan party and the gathering embitterment of his age, recapture the solid, healthful sweetness of his unpolitical youth. His genius did not stand still like Cowley's; it did not advance underground like Milton's; it simply became political. He was a poet who, perhaps, adapted his talent too easily to the circumstances of the time. True to his political views, he moved among the large, vocal opposition to the Court and used his pen in vivid satire. There is cruel skill in lines like those in which he mocks the desertion of the admiral and ships in the Medway by the courtiers.

Our feather'd gallants, which came down that day,
To be spectators safe of the new play,
Leave him alone when first they hear the gun;
(Cornbury the fleetest) and to London run. . . .

His contemptuous character of the King, in *The King's Vows*, puts into Charles's irreverent mouth the lines:

I will have a religion then all of my own,
Where Papist from Protestant shall not be known,
But if it grow troublesome I will have none.
I'll wholly abandon all public affairs,

And pass all my time with buffoons and players,
And saunter to Nelly when I should be at prayers.

It is vinegar-sharp, but what has happened to the lyric
grace of his youth, to the innocent and sensuous warmth
which created the lovely invocation *To His Coy Mistress*
or wrote on *Little T.C. in a prospect of Flowers*? Where
is the rich sweetness of the poet who lamented the lost
peace of England in the loveliest garden poem in the
language?

The separate developments of Marvell and Cowley
illustrate, in different ways, the tragedy of a whole
generation, the generation from which Milton alone,
puissant et solitaire, preserved his poetic soul entire and
lived to converse with archangels.

CHAPTER VIII

RESTORATION VERSE

WHILE MILTON trod his solitary path, the highroad of
English verse had turned in a different direction: towards
the couplet. It has been argued that the extravagances
of Cavalier poetry could have ended no other way, that
all this ingenuity and striving for effect, these far-sought
metaphors and extravagant conceits could only lead to a
reaction. The trim, explicit rhymed couplet was that
reaction.

This is rather too simple an explanation. Moreover it
is the explanation offered by those who see in the metaphysical period nothing more than the decadence of the
Elizabethan glory. If, on the other hand, one regards it
as a period of renewed rather than of decaying life, a
period of interesting and exciting experiment, a somewhat different pattern emerges. The rhymed couplet
was one of the many experiments tried by the fertile,
cliquish, competitive, Caroline poets. It was the one of
their many experiments which established itself as a permanent manner. It was not the reaction against them
but the surviving style they left behind.

A new generation of poets is usually disinclined to see
any resemblance between itself and its forebears. The
surviving *doyens* of the Cavalier epoch—Waller, Denham,
and Davenant—all vain men and all inferior poets, were
not likely to go about drawing attention to the rhymed

couplets of those who were dead and out of fashion. It was gratifying for them to be acclaimed by the younger men as the first of the reformers.

But the end-stopped couplet, complete in itself, did not begin with them. John Cleveland and Henry King both used it skilfully in their political poems; Cartwright was a master of it; Chalkhill's long narrative poem, *Thealma and Clearchus*, is in rhymed couplets varied only with slight irregularities, and Shackerley Marmion wrote the whole of his porcelain epic, *Cupid and Psyche*, in rhymed couplets, the sense being sometimes allowed to overflow from couplet to couplet, but often neatly imprisoned. George Sandys composed his translation of Ovid's *Metamorphosis* in rhymed, and often closed, couplets. Edward Fairfax in his translation of Tasso made some use of the form and Waller acknowledged his debt to him. There are innumerable other examples of the use of this form by the Caroline poets.

The reasons why the tripping, end-stopped pentameter survived all the other experiments were twofold. First, it is impossible to discount the influence of French poetry. All through the Cavalier period there was a constant interchange of ideas and influences with France. The dominating Spanish and Italian influences of the Jacobean age seemed old-fashioned. About 1630 the hairdressers, tailors, and dressmakers abandoned the constricting Spanish styles for the flowing, suggestive lines of the French mode. The women's stiffened, padded hair flowed into ringlets; the men defiantly adopted the pretty effeminacy of love-locks. Lovelace called on 'Amarantha sweet and fair' to 'braid no more thy shining hair'; but Donne's mistress, in going to bed, had disengaged herself from a coronet of wire. The indication of fashions is a sound one for the general tendencies of thought, and although in literary circles there was still talk of Lope da Vega and Calderón, of Guarini and Marino, although the individual influence of Spanish and Italian writers can be pointed out as late as 1700, the inescapable literary influence from the 1630s onwards was French. In France the rhymed couplet was the only wear.

The influences were still mingled among the Caroline poets. Sir Richard Fanshawe translated Guarini, and Crashaw much of Marino; Milton imbibed more Italian than French inspiration. But Katherine Philips, working away in Wales, had, before the Restoration, rendered Corneille's *Horace* into English couplets as self-contained and stiffly correct as any Academy could have wished. The plays of Corneille and of his numerous less remarkable contemporaries were widely known and read in England. They familiarized the educated with the peculiar merits of this form of poetic expression, above all with its trenchant clarity.

Politics was the second cause for the triumph of the couplet. The tide had already turned towards satirical and political verse before the Civil War broke out. In the latter half of the century political ideas and opinions were to dominate poetry as never before or since. The habit, already well established, of circulating poems among friends in manuscript lent itself to the secret dissemination of satire and propaganda. More could be said, more safely and more memorably, in verse than in prose.

The diffusion of newsletters and the growth of a considerable power of self-expression through all the literate classes was gradually extinguishing the spontaneous doggerel of broadsheet and ballad, which had enjoyed a brief St. Martin's summer during the war itself. There were some well-found variants on the old popular forms of the jaunty comic song—the mock litany, for instance:

> From an extempore prayer and a godly ditty,
> From the churlish government of a city,
> From the power of a country committee
>   *Libera nos, Domine.*

and that amiable device, to this day popular, of which 'The Clean Contrary Way' songs are typical. The game was to write a verse supposed to represent (while guying) the opposite point of view from that of the writer and to make the joke clear by the addition of 'the clean contrary way'.

> At Kineton, Brentford, Plymouth, York
> And divers places more
> What victories we Saints obtain
> The like ne'er seen before!
> How often we Prince Rupert killed
> And bravely won the day.
> The wicked Cavaliers did run
> The clean contrary way.

In the north, political passions could still strike out the sparks of spontaneous poetry and the narrative ballad flourished a little longer in Scotland and on the Borders before it went into lamentable decline. The *Bonnie House of Airlie*, the stirring *Haughs of Cromdale*, the hair-raising *Fire of Frendraught*, almost certainly *The Dowie Houms of Yarrow*, are of this time. In the south, political poetry was already growing more sophisticated, and only tales of murder and love, of monstrous births and sudden deaths were left to the anonymous ballad-mongers.

Political broadsheets were already displaying recognizable personal styles and manners which can in many cases be brought home to an author of distinction. John Cleveland contributed several; his powerful lines on Strafford have already been quoted.[1] A popular Royalist epitaph on Charles I, subsequently set to music by Samuel Pepys, was also attributed to him in error:

> Great, good and just, could I but rate
> My grief and thy too rigid fate
> I'd weep the world in such a strain
> That it should deluge once again.

There seems to be no doubt that the lines were the work of Montrose.

The most efficient of these political writers, however, devoted themselves whole-heartedly to their chosen sport. The anonymous hand of Sir John Mennes or the disreputable, indefatigable Marchamont Needham can be guessed at in many of these squibs and established with certainty in some. Needham's work has sometimes even been mistaken for that of Samuel Butler; it combines ruthlessness with a poetic imagination in much the same way. Thus he blisters the good name of the double-crossing Duke of Hamilton:

> Twas he patched up the new Divine
> Part Calvin and part Catiline.
> Rather than he his ends would miss
> Betray'd his Master with a kiss
> And buried in one common fate
> The glory of our Church and State.

The stream of political poetry, which had its origin in the tense atmosphere of London on the eve of the war, had become a steady river by the time of the Restoration.

---

[1] See *ante*, p. 82.

For this kind of expression the rhymed couplet is particularly suitable. It is easy to write—not well but well enough to pass—and it is relatively easy to say something sharp in it. It is also easily remembered. French models weighted the scales in favour of the more graceful line, the pentameter, instead of the lolloping octosyllabic verse to which Butler gave such vehemence in *Hudibras*. But it was political necessity which caused the triumph of the explicit, end-stopped couplet itself.

The three who claimed the credit deserve at least some of it. Denham's *Cooper's Hill*, published during the Civil War, is the work of a prosaic mind but can claim to have established a genre of topographical moralizing which in the hands of Goldsmith later reached a brief perfection. The lines on the Thames so warmly commended by Johnson in the ensuing century seem strangely flat to-day:

> O could I flow like thee and make thy stream
> My great example, as it is my theme!
> Tho' deep, yet clear; tho' gentle, yet not dull;
> Strong without rage, without o'er flowing full.

More interesting in the context of political poetry are his dignified lines on Strafford. Cleveland had used an unusual trochaic metre for this theme. Denham smooths out the tragedy into the elegant pentameter:

> Now private pity strove with public hate,
> Reason with rage, and eloquence with fate:
> Now they could him, if he could them forgive;
> He's not too guilty, but too wise to live.

After the Restoration his intellect acquired a certain feverish brilliance perhaps the result of private troubles. His young second wife became the Duke of York's mistress, a disaster which may have been responsible for the fit of insanity during which he 'went to the King, and told him he was the Holy Ghost'. In any case he recovered himself enough to write a fine elegy on Cowley's death, to survive his faithless wife who was alleged to have been poisoned in a cup of chocolate by the jealous Duchess of York, and to recognize the greatness of *Paradise Lost*. One or two savage satires of this period, once attributed to him, are not now regarded as his work.

Waller, acclaimed by Dryden as the man who perfected the English couplet, and certainly inclined to think of himself as such, is accomplished enough in his later poems in the heroic manner. But he rarely touched, in his elegant couplets, the spontaneous feeling or the flowing melody of the two most famous songs of his Cavalier period, 'Go, lovely rose' and 'On His Mistress' Girdle'. The same is true of the ambitious Davenant, self-styled laureate, most of whose mature pomposities are now generally forgotten, while his early and exquisite lyric, 'The lark now leaves her wat'ry nest', is rightly remembered.

The uncertainty of the final choice—whether for the four-foot line or the five-foot line—is well illustrated by that unique but far from irrelevant work, *Hudibras*. This poem is related as closely to the partly anonymous political literature that had preceded it as it is to the major political poetry of Dryden. The fragmentary masterpiece provides the missing link between the broadsheet poems of men like Needham and the sustained political passion of *Absalom and Achitophel*.

Hudibras is written in couplets of four feet to the line which are often but not always self-contained and where the sense invariably jumps with the metre. There is no interplay between the two; the scansion knocks the meaning on the head like a mallet knocking in pegs. The poem contains some reckless satire both political and social, a good deal of rather primitive knockabout, some memorable epigrammatic wisdom and much wonderfully skilled comic poetry. It breathes a cynical distrust of politics and religious fervour.

> When civil dudgeon first grew high
> And men fell out they knew not why;
> When hard words, jealousies and fears
> Set folks together by the ears,
> And made them fight, like mad or drunk,
> For Dame Religion, as for punk;
> Whose honesty they all durst swear for,
> Though not a man of them knew wherefore.

The opening is superb. So is the description of Hudibras himself, the corpulent and cowardly Presbyterian whose service to the cause gets him no further than a mistimed interference with a bear-baiting. But the poem breaks down for two reasons. Butler's passion is too spiteful; he loathes Hudibras, and although his loathing may have been both human and just, few great works of art can be carried through in hate alone. His model was *Don Quixote*, but he borrowed nothing from it except the idea of a modern knight-errant and a foolish attendant squire; the compassion of the Spaniard and his subtle and strong character-drawing are strangers to him. Possibly on account of his invincible distaste for his hero, he could not work out a satisfactory plot. After two lengthy adventures and an eloquent excursion into political satire, Butler gets tired of lambasting the fat knight, and the poem abruptly ends. There has been a good deal of laughter by the way and some wonderfully sharp comments on the follies of men—and chiefly of Presbyterians.

> A sect whose chief devotion lies
> In odd perverse antipathies;
> In falling out with that or this,
> And finding somewhat still amiss;
> More peevish, cross, and splenetic
> Than dog distract or monkey sick:
> That with more care keep holy day
> The wrong, than others the right way;
> Compound for sins they are inclined to,
> By damning those they have no mind to.
> Still so perverse and opposite
> As if they worshipped God for spite.

But the perusal of *Hudibras* fails altogether to impart that sense of added experience and knowledge that a great work of art can give.

Butler appears to have brought his fate as man and poet upon himself. He began his vituperative poem apparently while still living as a clerk in the house of pompous old Sir Samuel Luke (the supposed original of Hudibras) although, of course, he did not publish until after the Restoration. The first part of his poem gained him the admiration of the Court and of the King, but he was as cantankerous to those who favoured as to those who oppressed him and he seems to have died in the kind of poverty and half-neglect which overwhelms those who are their own worst enemies.

To move from Butler to Dryden is to move from the least polite to one of the most polite poets of the century. Yet their satire is often closely related. The angry contempt of *The Medal* is like nothing so much as certain

passages in *Hudibras*. Here Shaftesbury is far more
cruelly exposed than in *Absalom and Achitophel*:

> A vermin wriggling in the usurper's ear,
> Bartering his venal wit for sums of gold,
> He cast himself into the saint-like mould;
> Groaned, sighed and prayed, while godliness was gain,
> The loudest bag-pipe of the squeaking train.
> But as 'tis hard to cheat a juggler's eyes,
> His open lewdness he could ne'er disguise.
> There split the saint; for hypocritic zeal
> Allows no sins but those it can conceal.

John Dryden overshadows the last half of the seventeenth century as Ben Jonson did the Jacobean age. His
influence, paramount both in verse and prose, was even
more pervasive than that of his great predecessor. For
thirty years he was the established monarch of the literary
world, ruling it from his seat in Will's coffee-house as
Ben Jonson had done from his progression of taverns in
the Strand. Two influences could not have been more
comparable: two personalities could not have been more
different. The coffee-house and the park had replaced
the tavern as the meeting-place of the *literati*. Literature,
in form at least, was becoming polite; the process which
had begun at the Court of Charles I was completed
under the gentle and gentlemanly influence of Dryden.
Appearances, in the capital at least, now mattered more
than morals. The fashionable code of the time condoned
almost every vice but demanded a surface elegance that
sugared over the roughness of society although the aristocracy still set on their bravos to beat up their enemies
from time to time.

John Dryden, born in 1631, was a man of imperfect
character, of sometimes disingenuous morals, and some-

times vacillating will, but he had several remarkable qualities which Jonson lacked. He was genuinely modest and naturally generous in his estimate of other men's abilities. He established his influence by the evident superiority of his talent and maintained it without effort by the very gentleness of his rule. Certainly his enemies, at the height of his fame, felt the cutting edge of his tongue. In the venomous satire of *Mac Flecknoe* he flattened the rumbustious Shadwell who, with a kind of cheap-jack imitation of the Jonson manner, sought to rule the literary world. His politics began by swaying to the fashion of the Court: Cromwellian in 1658 when he saluted the Protector's death with a handsome elegy in the manner of Marvell; Cavalier in 1660 when he welcomed King Charles with the rather more individual *Astræa Redux*; High Tory by the end of the reign for the sequence of satires on the Whigs; Roman Catholic by 1686. But here, at the height of his powers and in the official position of Poet Laureate, his views remained fixed. When the Glorious Revolution brought the Whigs and William III to power, he made no compromise with the government. The braggart Shadwell took the Laureate's post from which his religion now disabled him. But official disfavour did not affect Dryden's unofficial position. It was indeed strengthened by the respect which men now felt for his dignity and constancy and he continued the unchallenged dictator of literary taste until his death in 1700.

Dryden was immensely prolific. His poems, plays, translations, essays, and letters, in the standard edition, fill eighteen volumes. He adapted Chaucer, Milton, and Shakespeare, translated from the French, the Latin and the Greek, wrote above twenty plays, nine long major poems, innumerable shorter works, and countless critical essays. With all this he found plentiful leisure to sit courteously at the feet of older poets when he was young and to advise younger ones when he was old.

Dryden's association with the heroic couplet—perfected in the eighteenth century to a cold and shining reasonableness—did his reputation harm with the Romantic school of critics. He was felt to belong to the Age of Reason and to have sacrificed warmth and passion to a perfected craftsmanship. But Dryden belongs wholly to the troubled and passionate seventeenth century. However different the surface of his work, his ways of thought were closer to those of Milton and closer to those of his Caroline predecessors than to those of Pope. In thought and phrase he echoes the metaphysical poets.

He has perhaps of all English poets the most varied and perfected technique. He studied it in prose and verse, in drama and narrative and satire, with almost religious care. This, allied to a particularly sensitive ear, gave him a mastery of poetic form and music which has rarely been equalled. But the lack of the supreme confidence which is a necessary concomitant (but unfortunately not a guarantee) of genius prevented him from ever quite doing what might be expected of him. In his anxiety to learn and his extraordinary facility for turning from one manner to another he was unique; but these very qualities prevented him from achieving the highest flight in anything that he did. There is always one scruple too much of the conscious artist in Dryden's work.

In his early narrative poems on State occasions and historic events—the Restoration, the Dutch wars, the Plague, the Fire—he steadily developed the flexibility and descriptive power of his verse. The last of the group, *Annus Mirabilis*, with its minute account of the Great Fire, marks the high-point of this kind of political-narrative poetry in English. The easy control of metre, imagery, and sense is impressive. The sly, crackling beginnings and the awful advance of the marauding flames is superbly described:

In this deep quiet, from what source unknown,
Those seeds of fire their fatal birth disclose;
And first few scattering sparks about were blown,
Big with the flames that to our ruin rose.

Then in some close-pent room it crept along
And, smouldering as it went, in silence fed;
Till the infant monster, with devouring strong,
Walked boldly upright with exalted head.

And now, no longer letted of his prey,
He leaps up at it with enraged desire,
O'er looks the neighbours with a wide survey,
And nods at every house his threatening fire.

At first they warm, then scorch, and then they bake;
Now with long necks from side to side they feed;
At length, grown strong, their mother-fire forsake,
And a new colony of flames succeed.

To every nobler portion of the town
The curling billows roll their restless tide;
In parties now they straggle up and down,
As armies unopposed for prey divide.

He turned from narrative poetry successively to the two poetic forms of drama, in blank verse and in rhyme. His blank-verse play, *All for Love*, is an experiment in the manner of Shakespeare and fails because he cannot create character and we are too often reminded of *Antony and Cleopatra* from which it derives. Were it possible to forget that, the blank verse of *All for Love* would stand a better chance of fair appraisal. It lacks the powerful originality of Milton's blank verse, but it is always dignified and sometimes moving.

The rhymed plays are more interesting, for in them it is possible to study Dryden's apprenticeship in the technique of the couplet. In the pastoral under-plot of *Marriage à la Mode*, he can run it off trippingly enough. How prettily the shepherdess-princess (a paste-board Perdita) recalls past joys to her swain:

> Do you remember, when their task was done
> How all the youth did to our cottage run?
> While winter winds were whistling loud without,
> Our cheerful hearth was circled round about;
> With strokes in ashes, maids their lovers drew;
> And still you fell to me, and I to you.

He attempted higher flights in *Aurengzebe* and *Almanzor and Almahide*, plays which contain lines of considerable beauty and passion in spite of the mockery which has been poured on them and for which Dryden's enemy, the malicious Duke of Buckingham, was largely responsible with his clever contemporary parody, *The Rehearsal*.

In 1681, with *Absalom and Achitophel*, Dryden followed Marvell and Butler into the field of political satire and at once gave the Court party a champion who could silence all opponents. Under the transparent disguise of a biblical story, Dryden described the faction created by the scheming Shaftesbury (Achitophel) round the vapid Duke of Monmouth. The savagely cruel descriptions of the false Achitophel himself and of Zimri (Dryden's old enemy Buckingham) are too famous to need quotation, but the poem glitters with a knife-edge brilliance throughout. For the King himself Dryden strikes for once a more simply humorous note:

> Then Israel's monarch after Heaven's own heart,
> His vigorous warmth did variously impart,
> To wives and slaves; and, wide as his command,
> Scatter'd his Maker's image thro' the Land.

Absalom and Achitophel was followed in 1682 by a second part, by *The Medal* and by *Mac Flecknoe* in which the poets of the opposing party are in turn exposed and dismissed.

This brief and eloquent jet of venom exhausted itself within two years. Dryden, as he grew older, was turning slowly towards philosophy and religion. In the same year, 1682, he wrote seriously on the Church of England in his *Religio Laici*. In the lovely *Elegy on Mrs. Anne Killigrew* the poet seems to suggest a new attitude to life.

> O gracious God! how far have we
> Profaned thy heavenly gift of poesy!
> Made prostitute and profligate the Muse,
> Debased to each obscene and impious use,
> Whose harmony was first ordained above,
> For tongues of angels and for hymns of love!

In *Religio Laici* and *The Hind and the Panther* he used the heroic couplet to express all that he felt or could feel about the eternal verities. What Dryden thought about the eternal verities was not particularly profound:

> Faith is not built on disquisitions vain;
> The things we must believe are few and plain.

But he believed what he believed sincerely and expressed his defence of the Anglican Church in *Religio Laici* and of the Roman Catholic Church in *The Hind and the*

Panther with a graceful, explicit skill. There is no sign of staleness in any of these poems and in 1700 he was still composing. 'What judgement I had increases rather than diminishes,' he wrote, 'and thoughts, such as they are, come crowding in so fast upon me, that my only difficulty is to choose or to reject, to run them into verse, or to give them the other harmony of prose.'

It was after his conversion to Catholicism that, writing for music, he attempted the complicated changing harmonies of his first and second *Ode for St. Cecilia's Day*. He himself preferred the later of the two, *Alexander's Feast*, or *The Power of Music*. But it is in the earlier ode that the wonderful lines on the dissolution of the world occur:

> As from the power of sacred lays
> The spheres began to move,
> And sung the great Creator's praise
> To all the blessed above;
> So when the last and dreadful hour
> This crumbling pageant shall devour,
> The trumpet shall be heard on high,
> The dead shall live, the living die,
> And Music shall untune the sky.

In its smooth certainty of touch it seems a long way from his metaphysical predecessors. But the quality of thought and feeling is the same; and the world of which Dryden writes is the same. The spheres make music, and the last trump rings out from 'round earth's imagined corners' with as dreadful a clangour as it did for Donne. In a manner that was to become the suave expression of the Augustan Age, John Dryden spoke the last vibrating messages of the age of conflict, faith, and redemption.

Beside Dryden the remaining Restoration poets seem more trivial even than they are. Congreve, a generation younger than Dryden, is the only comparable talent. Some of his incidental lyrics have a rare felicity, and in his verse tragedy, *The Mourning Bride*, there are passages of great technical accomplishment and some poetic fire.

The spring exuberance of the Cavaliers has given place to a blighted summer. The cult of the gentleman and courtier poet went on, but fertility and freshness had departed. There was a little facile skill, much imitation, much shameless robbery. Elkanah Settle, an uninteresting dramatist, lifted one of Fanshawe's prettiest lyrics to adorn one of his plays. The habit was a common one and has led unwary anthologists to give the credit to the wrong men. Most of them could, however, rhyme a pleasant lovesong, usually with some verbal felicity—like Sir Charles Sedley's pretty description of his yearnings and sufferings while (at the end of every verse):

> Phyllis, without frown or smile,
> Sat and knotted all the while.

The great translation tradition in English verse, distinguished by the Ovid of Sandys and the Tasso of Fairfax in the earlier part of the century, was carried on by the schoolmaster, Thomas Creech, who produced a light and accomplished version of Theocritus. John Oldham, who died young, pleasantly adapted some of the odes of Horace and followed in the footsteps of Cowley, though with less success, in essaying the Pindaric ode.

The Earl of Dorset added an engaging naval song, 'To all you ladies now on land', to the popular repertory. The Earl of Roscommon, regarded with respect by critics for a century after his death, wrote competent religious verses and died reciting one of them. The fantastic

Duchess of Newcastle, at once artless and highly metaphysical, scribbled away at her imaginative little poems
to the admiration of her elderly husband and the derision
of the world, leaving among other quaint fragments some
enchanting lines on a mermaid.

The Earl of Rochester had the makings of a great poet,
but he wasted his talent too often on monotonous impro-
prieties and ruined his health in debauch. Among his
remains there are lines of imaginative power and original
thought. His remarkable poem *On Nothing* recalls the
startled vision of Donne or Cowley, faced by the miracle
of a world created from nothing.

> Yet something did thy mighty pow'r command,
> And from thy fruitful Emptiness' hand,
> Snatch'd men, beasts, birds, fire, air and land.

He is bitter and acute when he compares Man with
Beasts in his *Satire against Mankind*:

> For Hunger or for Love they bite and tear
> Whilst wretched man is still in arms for Fear:
> For Fear he arms, and is of arms afraid;
> From Fear to Fear, successively betrayed,
> Base Fear, the source whence his best passions came,
> His boasted Honour and his dear-bought Fame.

To descend from the peerage, there is the buoyant Tom
d'Urfey who, in the snatches and catches that he wrote
for the Court or included in his plays, can often be
very pretty in a simple ballad manner. He plagiarized,
like most of his contemporaries, but he could achieve
what seems to be a genuine freshness. There is Philip
Ayres with his pretty emblem book of *amoretti* and
attendant verses. There is the late-born rural poet
Charles Cotton, a country gentleman with a turn for

verse, who had known Lovelace in his youth and was a friend and collaborator of Izaak Walton in his maturity. Sometimes he wrote the usual love-lyrics, but on occasion he could rhyme about the country with easy natural observation which is far from being great poetry, but has a style and humour of its own. His incidental pieces in *The Compleat Angler* are charming, and his quatrains on the different times of day are full of homely observation.

He conveys with artless precision the atmosphere of evening on the busy farm:

> The cock now to the roost is prest,
> For he must call up all the rest;
> The sow's fast pegg'd within the sty,
> To still her squeaking progeny.
>
> Each one has had his supping mess,
> The cheese is put into the press,
> The pans and bowls clean scalded all,
> Rear'd up against the milk-house wall.

Far away from the Court and London, further far than Charles Cotton, a few untutored poetic talents bloomed unnoticed, or unnoticed by the literary world. Thomas Traherne, whose exquisite prose became famous only in this century, left a sheaf of religious poems which have the same quality of innocent, inquiring wonder. John Bunyan, writing for the unlettered and for children, made, now and again, from unassuming doggerel, a phrase or a couplet that holds its own against time. Among the glad-hearted Quakers doggerel hymns were frequent too. Some of them were touching, profound, or beautiful. There was more learning and city elegance in the metrical version of the psalms prepared by Nicholas Brady and Nahum Tate who had been a successful playwright and the collaborator of Dryden.

But English poetry as the century drew to its close was no longer the hubbub of more or less tuneful voices which it had been sixty years before. The scene which the aged Dryden courteously dominated as he sipped his coffee at Will's was an England in which prose had acquired the ease and vigour and variety which had gradually been drained from poetry; but it was, above all, a place of greater literary reticence. Reticence can be a virtue in literature but it is a cramping one. It was perhaps the only virtue that the outspoken, fertile seventeenth century did not possess.

CHAPTER IX

THE THEATRE AFTER 1660

THE DEVELOPMENT of the Restoration theatre out of its Jacobean and Caroline predecessors was more continuous than might have been expected from the events of the political world or the social scene. In 1642 the London theatres were closed, to be unofficially and temporarily reopened in 1648, officially permitted under a limited licence in 1656, and fully restored in 1660.

During the interval some of the actors had performed in private houses or surreptitiously even in theatres; the acting tradition was thus unbroken and the boys who had played Juliet and Annabella came back in 1660 to play the male leads. The women's parts were henceforward taken by women, a change which had been long on its way. A French company with women players had performed in London during the 'thirties and had already broken down some of the prejudice against them. Ladies, after all, not infrequently performed in masques. Why not, therefore, on the stage? The public during the Commonwealth had read with greed every printed play on which it could lay hands. The theatre habit was too strong among the English to be so lightly killed, nor were the Puritans by any means unanimously opposed to it. At Cromwell's Courts there were occasional pastorals— Marvell's, for instance, for the wedding of the Protector's daughter—and it may be safely presumed that private theatricals were still frequent about the country.

The commonly held but misleading belief that the closing of the theatres broke the continuity of dramatic developments has been confirmed by the loose habit of calling all drama up to 1642 'Elizabethan', or at best 'Jacobean', and all drama after 1660 'Restoration', although there is nothing Elizabethan and not much Jacobean about the distinctively Caroline work of Shirley, Cartwright, or Carlell, who wrote in the 'thirties; and nothing particularly Restoration about Congreve, Vanbrugh, or Farquhar, all of whom are depicting the settled post-Revolution society of King William III. These are terms which need modification if the richest century of the English theatre is to be understood at all.

Comedy in the seventeenth century describes a continuous movement—with incidental variations—from the Comedy of Humours which was Jonson's development of the old morality play, to the Comedy of Manners which, in a thin and decadent form, survived almost to the present time. The downward movement of tragedy is, unhappily, also continuous; in spite of the conflagration at the beginning of the century and the unexpected flash of Thomas Otway in the 'eighties, the English genius seems at once too humorous and too humane for tragedy. Common sense will keep breaking in. Even Dryden thought that Hippolytus in Racine's *Phèdre* was a perfect fool rather than a perfect hero. The result was a steady decline from the thundering magnificence of the Elizabethans to the refined boredom of the Augustan Age. The almost unreadable tragedies of Nicholas Rowe and his contemporaries are thin-blooded descendants of those of Webster, Middleton, and Ford:

the ghost of Jacobean drama sitting crowned on the grave thereof.

More significant than the closing of the theatres for fourteen years was the gradual change in the composition of the public. The increase of a more rabid Puritanism among craftsmen and small tradespeople even before the theatres closed had altered the social character of the audience; the London theatres continued to be supported after the Restoration, as during the 'thirties, by the more cultivated bourgeoisie, the aristocracy, and their innumerable hangers-on. Before 1642 it had been usual for the King to send for the players to Whitehall, although Queen Henrietta Maria had been unconventional enough, once at least, to attend the theatre in person. Her son, Charles II, with his easy delight in plays and players, established the custom of the royal box at Drury Lane.

Before the Civil War broke out playwrights were already moving away from the once popular scenes of apprentice and City life towards those of wealth and fashion. It is, however, an exaggeration to suggest that Restoration drama concentrated on the Court set even during the period when the Court were ardent theatregoers. In Etherege and Wycherley as well as in the later Congreve and Vanbrugh the society depicted touches only the edge of the Court circle and is based on a wider circle of the wealthy, the intelligentsia, the wits, who formed the influential part of the audience.

The type of comedy which pleased them most was concerned exclusively with the pursuit of women by men and of men by women; no moral was now added—as in Shirley or Brome—to sweeten the ending; marriage and fidelity are usually mocked, although conventional marriages do occur to end some of these plays and there is by no means always a suggestion that they will be ephemeral. Virtuous characters are rare, but not, as some critics sweepingly suggest, wholly absent. Congreve's three chief heroines, Cynthia, Angelica, and Millamant, are not merely above suspicion, but even cold. Wycherley has his Alethea, his more dubious Fidelia, and an earlier heroine, Hippolyta, is a gay but not a bad girl. The dialogue aims at great verbal wit but at obscenity chiefly by innuendo. It is more polished and far less openly coarse than that of the earlier period.

'He assured me your ladyship should come to no damage,' pleads Lady Wishfort's maid to her mistress as an excuse for her plot to palm off the footman on her as an aristocratic lover. 'No damage?' shrieks the outraged old harridan. Lady Wishfort and her maid would have used plainer English fifty years before and would have raised a less delighted laugh.

The taste of the period was, however, by no means stilted. Revivals of the older drama were frequent, and veteran playgoers must have appreciated the nuances of difference in the familiar scenes which came from the introduction of more complex effects and the appearance of women players. Margaret Hughes, one of the first recorded tragediennes, made her reputation as a gentle ash-blonde Desdemona. Her fame paled before that of the passionate Mrs. Barry, for whom the love-sick Otway wrote all his greatest female parts. Certainly with the women players and the open erotic attachments which now existed between the audience and the stage, the fashion of writing parts to suit specific talents much increased. Mechanical aids which had begun under Charles I developed steadily under his son. The veteran

Davenant believed in the spectacular; he had been about to build a theatre for elaborate, operatic shows before the war came, and in 1656 he received his licence from Cromwell and introduced the new art of opera to England with *The Siege of Rhodes.*

Apart from the new taste for more music and more scenery many of the plays produced during the last forty years of the seventeenth century are still closely akin to the earlier models. Tuke's untidy *Adventures of Five Hours*, d'Urfey's sprawling gallery of adaptations from novels and histories, Lacy's light-hearted Civil War comedy, *The Old Troop*, are all close to the past traditions of the English theatre. Thomas Shadwell, a prolific playwright of the 'eighties, modelled himself frankly on Ben Jonson (although he could find time to refurbish Shakespeare as well). In his comedies, *The Squire of Alsatia* and the gaily provincial *Bury Fair*, he followed out the formula of the comedy of humours with competent, if mechanical, characterization and lively dialogue.

The playwrights with whom the new age opened, Tom Killigrew, George Etherege, John Crowne, John Lacy, and the fashionable rake Sir Charles Sedley, all treated their characters in the Jonsonian manner and created theatrical versions of one or two social types which were to become recurrent in Restoration comedy. John Crowne's fop, Sir Courtly Nice, is closely followed by Etherege's Sir Fopling Flutter, from whom descends, among a host of lesser fops, Vanbrugh's Lord Foppington. Etherege's country girl, Miss Harriet, is a charming first sketch for the less charming, more memorable Miss Prue and Miss Hoyden with whom Congreve and Vanbrugh followed. Dryden perhaps alone of these earlier writers tried, not altogether successfully, to maintain the pastoral note in comedy and to handle character with greater subtlety of light and shade. But neither his *Wild Gallant* nor his *Marriage à la Mode* altogether succeed in combining the old romance with the new cynicism.

The theatres which opened in 1660 were no longer on the old model, with the apron stage and the audience crowding close to the players. They were now built on the French model, with a picture stage framed in the proscenium arch and the audience separated from it and grouped in a semi-circular building in front of and above it. The Court had not long resettled at Whitehall before French comedy became the talk of the day. The precise influence of French models is a matter of dispute. English drama had already deeper and tougher roots than French drama, and French classical tragedy almost instantaneously provoked English derision. Although the rhymed couplet was for a while tried out on the stage, the fundamentals of English tragedy always remained much closer to the Elizabethan; passion and action could not or would not be forced into the French mould.

In comedy the relations between the English and the French stage were rather different. While almost all English dramatists mocked the unities and preferred to follow the old method of an untidy naturalism, they saw no objection to stealing any plot that took their fancy. It was unfortunate on the whole that they used Molière as their chief source, because comparisons were later bound to be made which would be to their discredit. It is kinder and fairer to forget *Le Misanthrope* and *L'Ecole des Femmes* when considering *The Plain Dealer* or *The Country Wife*, which have nothing to do with the French except that Wycherley took a fancy to the stories. Barefaced robberies of plot and situation continued over the whole of this period, but the influence which this represents was skin deep. Originality was not the strong point of any of these playwrights and they pillaged their own dead countrymen for phrases and situations as unscrupulously as they did the French. Sedley's best scene in *Bellamira* is merely an adaptation of the great Falstaff scene with eleven men in buckram.

The wrong-headed, neurotic Wycherley is the first great comic dramatist after the Restoration. His quality is very hard to estimate on the four plays which were all that he left. Possibly he was an Elizabethan out of place and would have done less startling but more satisfying work had he been able to vent his impotent rage against mankind in the manner of his predecessors. His first play, *Love in a Wood*, is a brisk piece of nonsense about philandering pairs and mistaken identities in St. James's Park. His second play, *The Gentleman Dancing Master*, has a purely Jonsonian character in the tyrannous old father whose humour it is always to be in the right, a foible which in the end compels him to pretend that he has known all along about his daughter's intrigue with the hero and had always intended to have him for a son-in-law.

In the unmitigated brutality of *The Plain Dealer* and the satirical violence of *The Country Wife* the savage Wycherley at last breaks through. Where Molière's Misanthrope is a character very nearly tragic in the intensity of his feelings, Wycherley's plain-dealer, Manly, is merely odious, a boor who thinks himself better than others because he makes no attempt to conceal his feelings. It is never clear—a serious fault in drama—whether Wycherley himself condones Manly's conduct, which is throughout repulsive if frank. This smag and selfish savage who imagines himself superior to others merely because he is ruder may have been Wycherley's conception of himself. The frequent coupling of the words 'manly Wycherley' by his contemporaries when they spoke of him suggests that this was known to be so. This unpleasing but undeniably striking play contains a scene satirizing the scandal-mongering conversation of women which was lifted and adapted by Sheridan for *The School for Scandal*. Wycherley's final capitulation to the manners of his time was signalized by his last and best play, *The Country Wife*.[1] This work, which scandalized even the London of 1672, amounts in fact to a violent statement (in the wittiest terms) that if society wishes to go to hell in its own way, it can go for all Wycherley cares. Hence the elaborate concluding scene in which husbands and wives consent to remain the dupes or accessories of Mr. Horner's indelicate make-believe. Regarded neither as satire nor as comedy is it a pleasant play, but the characters are conceived with a gusto which, for once, Jonson could not have surpassed, and in dialogue and situation it still remains one of the funniest and most rewarding comedies in the language.

Very soon after the appearance of Wycherley's comedies, the tragedies of Thomas Otway took the stage. Otway, whose *Venice Preserv'd* was regularly revived until the beginning of the nineteenth century, is the last English tragic dramatist of any real moment, in spite of the contemporary neglect of his work. Otway's verse, it is true, lacks the youthful splendour of his Elizabethan fore-

[1] *The Plain Dealer* was rewritten and slightly altered after the production of *The Country Wife*, chiefly to include a scene in which the hypocritical Olivia may characterize *The Country Wife* as 'filthy'. It is, however, substantially the earlier play.

runners, but it is often moving and never feeble. His characters are convincing and his sense of theatre is considerable. Moreover, he had a real conception of the tragic in life; his catastrophes occur because of 'what is false within'. His heroes and heroines, usually the weak and the well-meaning, bring disaster on themselves and on those they love. Don Carlos in the play of that name and, above all, Jaffir in *Venice Preserv'd* are sensitive studies of decent, honourable men vacillating in the grip of passions or problems which are beyond them. Belvidera, the heroine of *Venice Preserv'd*, who incites her husband to betray his friends and goes out of her mind after he has committed suicide, is an unusually fine study of a woman too set upon her own way to realize what its consequences may be to the man she loves. Her mad scene, cruelly parodied by Sheridan in *The Critic*, is funny enough if snatched out of its context, but in its place in the play is dramatically effective and psychologically probable. Otway's was a young talent, still maturing when he died at the age of just over thirty, some say of hunger and some of love for Mrs. Barry. Whatever the circumstances of poor Otway's death—and enough is known of his sensibility and his sufferings to justify the adjective 'poor'—it robbed English drama of a potentially great tragic writer.

Dryden's three tragedies, of about the same time, are inferior to Otway's both in characterization and drama. Tragedy in the grand manner, and Dryden in particular, was satirized in the Duke of Buckingham's clever squib, *The Rehearsal*, a popular piece of erudite impertinence which Sheridan used as the basis for his better known *The Critic*. No other dramatist need be seriously mentioned. That interesting woman writer, Mrs. Aphra Behn, provided the stage with numerous tedious and pretentious dramas; her real talent lay elsewhere. Nathaniel Lee and Nicholas Rowe who bring up the rear are deservedly as dead as Queen Anne, although it was Rowe who gave to the language the expression 'gay Lothario'. At least it was Rowe who wrote *The Fair Penitent* in which it occurs. The play is very loosely based on Massinger's *Fatal Dowry* and tells of a young woman, Calista, who, seduced by her husband's friend Lothario just before her marriage, attempts in vain to keep the secret of her crime. Weak as the play is, it provided in Calista a favourite part for Mrs. Siddons, and in Lothario a model from which the novelist, Samuel Richardson, must have drawn inspiration for the most attractive blackguard in fiction, the Lovelace of *Clarissa Harlowe*.

Dilettantism—which, to begin with, had added a certain freshness to comedy—was probably in the end its undoing. Too many witty young men, from 1630 onwards, were diluting the professional manner with their more frivolous attempts. From dilettantism it is a short step to mere frivolity. In Vanbrugh this is already apparent. He took no trouble at all. Because he had high spirits, a sense of character and theatre, and an inventive wit, he wrote remarkably entertaining plays none the less: his *Relapse* and his *Provoked Wife* can still comfortably hold the modern stage. He abandoned the theatre at a comparatively early age for architecture. Farquhar, equally gay and amateurish when he began to write for the stage, was finding himself as a dramatist of manners, and a conscientious artist in dialogue and character before he died. His *Constant Couple* and *Recruiting Officer* are comedy trembling on the brink of farce, although the character of Sir Harry Wildair in the first is one of the great creations of English dramatic fiction; of all the high-spirited rakes of the period, Mirabell included, Wildair is by far the most attractive and the most convincing. In his last play, *The Beaux' Stratagem*, Farquhar is on the way to no less witty but more solid comedy of manners. His early death cut off what might have been a valuable development.

The outstanding dramatist of the closing decade of the century is William Congreve. It would be easy to make too much of this figure of Congreve, who abandoned the career of a dramatist at thirty, and precisely in the year 1700, for the more pleasing business of leading a civilized and cultured life between his residence and the coffee-houses. There is a certain significance about this, and it is probably not by chance that the only comparable dramatist in the next two centuries, Sheridan, also wrote his comedies before he was thirty—and for fun. Serious creative literature was turning away from drama towards the novel.

The reputation of Congreve has never quite stabilized. In his own time he was rated in terms that must be regarded as too high. He combined, wrote one critic, 'Shakespeare's wit and Jonson's oil'. Dryden, a good judge, declared that

Heaven, that but once was prodigal before,
To Shakespeare gave as much: she could not give him
    more.

It was generally felt, as the century drew to its close, that in other spheres beside the drama

When Dryden goes, 'tis he must fill the chair,
With Congreve only Congreve can compare.

But the bright talent for writing evaporated into a

talent for talking. After his fifth play, *The Way of the World*, he scarcely wrote again. His first play, *The Old Batchelor*, is a gay comedy of intrigue, still Jonsonian in conception but remarkable for the epigrammatic wit of the dialogue. His second play, *The Double Dealer*, has a strangely tragic underplot which disturbs the balance of an otherwise dexterous comedy of manners, full of cleverly drawn characters, conceived, sometimes from recognizable living models, as individuals and not merely as 'humours'; the affected Lady Froth,[1] the doting Sir Paul Plyant, the vain Mr. Brisk. But the passionate ageing Lady Touchwood and her jealous husband are too painfully real for comedy. Congreve drew character too well to be able to keep such figures within the convention of comedy, as the less subtle Wycherley so easily could. When at the close Lady Touchwood—all her plots discovered—hurls herself across the stage in an agony of despair with her angry husband in pursuit, the fragile walls of comedy crack to pieces. 'This is all very extraordinary, let me perish!' exclaims little Mr. Brisk in an effort to preserve the gaiety of mood and bring down a more seemly curtain. But he cannot save his author.

Yet in *The Mourning Bride* Congreve showed that he could not sustain high tragedy. Had fashion allowed him to write tragedy in prose, perhaps it would have been different; he had been very near to it in parts of *The Double Dealer*. But his verse is too conscious and his conception of character outside the world he knew and lived in, too stilted.

His fame stands, and on the whole securely, on *Love for Love* and *The Way of the World*. In both of these he

---

[1] Probably a portrait of the Duchess of Newcastle. See *ante*, pp. 136–7.

develops not the comedy of humours, but the naturalist comedy of manners. Certain characters—Miss Prue, Sir Sampson Legend, Witwoud—approximate to existing types, but they are endowed with strong individuality of their own. The drama—in spite of a good deal of extraneous plot—is provided by the interplay of the characters who are seen wonderfully in the round. Congreve, in the capacity to suggest the human tragedy behind the human comedy, is the only writer of this time who can be compared with Molière. There is a profound comment on social customs and on human character in the drawing of Valentine, the young man brought up to enjoy private means and suddenly disinherited; and his father, Sir Sampson Legend, approaches nearer to implied tragedy than to farce in the grandeur of his self-conceit and the absurdity of his courting of his son's beloved, the young Angelica. Each character is drawn so as to convey a whole life *off* the stage as well as on it.

In *Love for Love* Congreve has painted a fairly comprehensive piece in which a number of human and social problems are kept moving all the time. In *The Way of the World* the focus is much narrower. The centre of interest is the duel of wits between Millamant and Mirabell; the surrounding society merely reflects aspects of the battle royal between them; the faithless husband Fainall, the jilted Mrs. Marwood and the ageing Lady Wishfort, serve dramatically to heighten the horrid possibilities latent in the situation between Millamant and Mirabell. These two are not on a level with the merry quarrelling young lovers of Elizabethan comedy. They are the civilized man and the civilized woman working out move by move and step by step, in the wittiest language and with an appearance of great confidence, the insoluble problem of how to deal with an animal passion in a sophisticated world.

This background to the social morals of the period should not be forgotten. The old system of chivalry, in which women were chattels—precious chattels, but chattels none the less—to be protected and possessed had in an attenuated form governed the moral outlook of the upper classes well into the seventeenth century. A new morality had not yet been worked out to fit a society which had finally come unmoored from feudalism and chivalry. With all their cynicism, the morals of the fast set in the later seventeenth century represent a move towards greater justice between men and women. The capacity to meet a man on equal terms, which had been the prerogative of an occasional Brunhild or Britomart, was now open to any woman of quick wits. It can hardly be sustained that the morality depicted by Wycherley, Etherege, Congreve, and Vanbrugh is an advance on that depicted by Spenser, Shakespeare, Massinger, or even Ford. But at least theirs is a society in which neither Hero nor Imogen could be so scandalously mistreated by their lovers with the full approval of society. The excesses of a comparatively small set of men and women, and of the comedies which depicted them, were the price paid for a steady social advance.

Two years before the appearance of *The Way of the World*, in 1698, Jeremy Collier published his *Short View of the Immorality and Profaneness of the English Stage*. This naïve outpouring, by a clergyman who was not much of a theatregoer, succeeded by only a few years a parallel outburst by Thomas Rymer, the lawyer and antiquary, some of whose ideas it reproduces. Collier's vituperation startled public opinion. Proceedings for indecency were started against d'Urfey and Congreve himself. The reverend gentleman had spent his time (most unsuitably 'for one of his function', as Dryden pointed out) combing the printed editions of plays for their depravities, and his book contains an exhaustive list of where these are to be found—title, author, act, scene, and line—very convenient for those who are interested in such things. The fatuous old snob was as much incensed by mockery of the upper classes as he was by bawdy jokes. 'They kick the coronets about the stage', he protested explosively, meaning that Vanbrugh and others had depicted members of the peerage as the tricksters and fools that some of them undoubtedly were.

There was at one time an inclination to believe that English comedy died of the shock administered by Jeremy Collier's attack. This is hardly true, for Vanbrugh, d'Urfey, Congreve, and Farquhar shortly resumed writing without undue embarrassment. But they were the last in the great tradition of English comedy. Collier's attack merely voiced what was being felt fairly widely in literate society because the robust fashion in the theatre had exhausted itself. The fierce wind of genius no longer filled the sails of English drama; under the insipid influence of Rowe and Addison and Colley Cibber it was long to ride becalmed 'a painted ship upon a painted ocean'.

The development of easy, flexible prose and the Puritan prejudice which overhung the provinces and the commercial middle classes together forced the English inventive genius to find another outlet. Men who, in 1600, would have hastened to London to write for the stage, now found the means to reach an even wider public in a manner which was not condemned by the classes from which most of them came. This was the novel. A butcher's son, of Nonconformist background, Daniel Foe, had been born nine years before Congreve; he changed his name to Defoe in 1702. His late-maturing talent, expended on pamphleteering, did not find its outlet in *Robinson Crusoe* until 1719. To him and his like came the dramatic heritage of the English creative genius. The novel, the outcast of the seventeenth century, was to be the glory of the eighteenth.

CHAPTER X

THE LATER EVOLUTION OF PROSE

ALL THIS time English prose had been steadily increasing in scope and power. The causes were clear enough. The multitudinous new interests and new experiments of the century needed to be recorded, while the spread of a kind of minor education—the ability to read and write—to thousands who would never have leisure or interest to acquire Latin made it necessary that most books should now be written in English. Technical knowledge was increasing and technical knowledge cannot be imparted in Italian rhetoric. Without realizing what they were doing, without intending to do it, the hundreds of gifted craftsmen, successful farmers, enthusiastic ship-builders, skilled seamen, and practised sportsmen who sat down to write such books as *The Seaman's Grammar, The Young Sportsman's Instructor, Observations and Improvements in Husbandry, A New Discovery of the Old Art of Teaching School,* and others were creating a new English prose. It is seen at its best perhaps in such eminently sensible works as Josiah Child's study in political economy, *A New Discourse of Trade,* or Hezekiah Woodward's serious and gentle pamphlets on the education of the young.

This kind of writing, and the growth of a written colloquial language, partly the result of the Civil War, were the two most decisive influences on the modern English prose which came into being in the latter half of the century. A rich afterglow yet lingered from the earlier styles. The most extraordinary of the pedantic writers of English died in 1660, not without having left behind one remarkable monument of literature. Sir Thomas Urquhart of Cromarty was a Scot; he was also an eccentric whose considerable learning ran to seed in a peculiar fashion. He was absorbed in words, not, like Florio, because he felt the practical need for new and more exact or expressive words—although he felt that too and made plentiful use of Cotgrave's French-English dictionary—but because he liked piling the borrowed syllables up into jaw-breakers. He wrenched new words from the Latin, the Greek, and the Hebrew and hurled them in unreadable sentences, containing incomprehensible ideas, at a stunned or indifferent public. 'Betwixt what is printed and what is ready for the press,' he wrote, 'I have set forth above a hundred several books, on subjects never hitherto thought upon by any.' Typically, these included *Logopandecteision, or an Introduction to the Universal Language.* He worked away with useless patience and vain learning at one lunatic invention after another, quarrelled verbosely with everyone who contradicted him, flung himself on a sudden surge of loyalty into the armies of King Charles II, and lost two trunks full of manuscripts when he was taken prisoner after the battle of Worcester. Every now and again in the torrential flow of verbosity, the waters part and there is a green island of charm and good sense. To him we owe that excellent character of the Admirable Crichton, and a description of the mathematician Napier of Merchistoun by which his personality has found immortality as well as his logarithms. But Urquhart is a writer to be tasted chiefly in selections.

Yet once his patience settled upon the right object. He translated Rabelais, and the Rabelais-Urquhart combination is a masterpiece comparable with that earlier miracle of Montaigne-Florio. Urquhart, like Florio, occasionally mistranslated, and like Florio, only with more exuberance, he absorbed and transformed his original. For one thing he made it nearly a quarter as long again. Give Urquhart a good thing, and he could not let it alone; if Rabelais offers six alternatives (and Rabelais had a great way of building up catalogues) Urquhart will make it sixteen. Thus the cake-bakers of Lerné, when they turned upon the importunate shepherds of Gargantua's country, not only called them more bad names than the twenty-nine allowed to them by Rabelais, but showed themselves also masterly inventors of abuse, for they 'did injure them most outrageously, calling them prattling gabblers, drowsy loiterers, slap-sauce fellows, slabber degullion druggels, lubbardly louts, drawlatch hoydens, scurvy sneaksbies, fondling fops, blockish grutnols, doddi-pol jolt-heads, jobbernol goose-caps, lob dotterels, ninny-hammer flycatchers, noddie-peak simpletons . . .' And so on and so on. Urquhart's Rabelais is a rich, juicy, eccentric, extraordinary book, as succulent as the original, a great bursting haggis of a book.

A talent comparable to, and a mind greater than, that of Urquhart belonged to his contemporary Sir Thomas Browne, the Norwich physician. Browne shared Urquhart's passion for manufacturing words derived from the Latin and Greek, but was a great deal more sane. He was nearer in feeling to Burton, whose technique in stringing together the results of wide and anecdotal reading he partly shared. The logic of his deductions, whether philosophic or scientific, belongs already to the age of the Royal Society, and his deep religious preoccupation places him high among the meditative writers of the century. The range and discipline of his mind is evident even in that voluminous compilation which he made to refute certain *Vulgar Errors*. It is much more true of his most famous work, *Religio Medici*, in which he set down the honest considerations of a thoughtful man on faith, morality, and conduct. It is a unique mixture of logic and imagination, attractive in its matter and manner but most of all for the imaginative grasp of the mind which its paragraphs gradually reveal. Thus, for instance, he writes of his body and of the world:

Now for my life it is a miracle of thirty years, which to relate were not a history, but a piece of poetry, and would sound to common ears like a fable. For the world, I count it not an inn, but an hospital; and a place not to live but to die in. The world that I regard is myself; it is the microcosm of my own frame that I cast mine eye on: for the other, I use it like my globe, and turn it round sometimes for my recreation. Men that look upon my outside, perusing only my condition and fortunes, do err in my altitude; for I am above Atlas' shoulders.

Religio Medici was written just before the Civil War. Connoisseurs of Browne—like Burton he has his connoisseurs—prefer the perfected style of *Hydriotaphia, or Urn Burial* which did not appear until 1658. In this work Browne discusses burial customs in a series of learned reflections arising from the excavation of an ancient repository of human ashes in his neighbourhood. In its rich and subtle use of words, rhythms, and alliterations, in its inventive and striking descriptions, it reaches again and again to moments of a rich and singular beauty.

Now since these dead bones have already out-lasted the living ones of Methusaleh, and in a yard underground, and thin walls of clay, out-worn all the strong and spacious buildings above it; and quietly rested under the drums and tramplings of three conquests: what prince can promise diuturnity unto his relics, or might not gladly say,

Sic ego componi versus in ossa velim?

Time, which antiquates antiquities, and hath an art to make dust of all things, hath yet spared these minor monuments. In vain we hope to be known by open and visible conservatories, when to be unknown was the means of their continuation, and obscurity their protection.

'What prince can promise such diuturnity . . .' But the time for linguistic virtuosity was fast going by. Hobbes, writing at the same time of political theory, is dry and wiry.

Practical prose, the antithesis of Urquhart's and Browne's, received a kind of official charter of gentility with the foundation of the Royal Society in 1660. It was decided that the deliberations and transactions of this learned body should be printed in English. Its eminent secretary, John Evelyn, and its first historian, Bishop Sprat, provide examples of the clear, well-mannered prose which all its members aimed at. Evelyn's considerable output of works on natural history do not ever achieve quite the rank of great literature, but the style even of his instructions to his gardener is a model of exactness and charm.

The Gardiner should walk about the whole Gardens every Monday morning duly, not omitting the least corner, and so observe what flowers or trees or plants want staking, binding and redressing or are in danger;

especially after great storms and high winds and then immediately to reform, establish, shade, water etc. what he finds amiss, before he go about any other work.

Bishop Sprat, on the whole, has less charm than Evelyn but he says what he has to say with a concise diction which has its claim to a place in literature.

To this fault of sceptical doubting, the Royal Society may perhaps be suspected to be a little too much inclin'd; because they always professed to be so backward from settling of principles or fixing upon doctrines. But if we fairly consider their intentions, we shall soon acquit them. Though they are not yet very daring in establishing conclusions; yet they lay no injunctions upon their successors not to do the same, when they shall have got a sufficient store for such a work. It is their study, that the way to attain a solid speculation should every day be more and more pursued; which is to be done by a long forbearing of speculation at first, till the matters be ripe for it; and not by madly rushing upon it in the very beginning.

If there is nothing very original in this style, it flows smoothly, is crystal clear, and avoids at once the obvious and the ornate.

While the new practical prose came into being among the men of learning, a revolt against the overcharged prose of the Jacobean age had also begun in another quarter, if a movement so quiet can be thought of as a revolt. The colloquial style, already developed in private letters and diaries during the first half of the seventeenth century, had appeared in at least two works of literature, written before the Civil War although not published until after. George Herbert, in the tranquillity of his vicarage at Bemerton, had composed a short handbook, *A Priest to the Temple*, for the advice of the clergy. Since this work is in a sense simply a professional guide, it is perhaps not surprising to find that it partakes so much in style of the unvarnished quality of the craftsman's manual.

Izaak Walton, who wrote Herbert's life, probably did not finish his more famous *Compleat Angler* until after the half-century, but some of his *Lives* of contemporary writers were composed rather earlier. The long life of this philosophic and well-read London ironmonger covers almost the whole of the century. He was about twenty-five when he became the friend of Donne in whose *Life* Sir Henry Wotton later asked him to collaborate. Walton, who had known everyone from Drayton onwards, lived until 1683. His style therefore may have had time to alter with fashion, but it is more probable that he was both a natural and original stylist. He wrote as he spoke, with a measured simplicity, always suited to the occasion. His unaffected treatment of the subjects of his biographies compares rather startlingly with the pompous style usually employed by the biographers of the earlier seventeenth century. This was the period at which the skies never did less than dissolve in tears for every death lamented in contemporary elegy, and prose tributes strove to out-top adjective by adjective in a style of heightened eulogy, so that Walton's gentle, unaffected narratives are all the more impressive. Gaiety and humanity he has always; humour he seems occasionally to lack. The picture which concludes his life of Herbert, that of Mrs. Herbert drawing the attention of her second husband to the exalted merit of her first, is not perhaps so attractive as Walton seems to think.

In general the lives are, however, inferior to *The Compleat Angler*, where Walton had a subject that exactly suited his unpretentious ambling manner. There is nothing else in the English language quite like these pleasant, instructive dialogues with their atmosphere of green meadows, happy streams, and quiet inn parlours. There is a touch of a less donnish Burton, a good deal of the practical quality of the seventeenth-century hand-book, but most of all of Walton's genial, conversational humour, his vivid apprehension of landscape and simple pleasures.

Jeremy Taylor's wholesome, sweet, and sensible *Holy Living* and *Holy Dying* have not the simplicity of Herbert's practical advice to the country clergy; but the two books, and Taylor's other work, show the highly-wrought philosophic prose of the earlier period well on its way to an easier simplicity. Both he and that other great contemplative, Traherne, whose *Centuries of Meditations* were first printed only in 1908, have a delicate sensitivity to the beauty of the world akin to that of the best of the Cavalier poets. Thus Jeremy Taylor, developing the old simile of the bubble for man's life, writes: 'the young man dances like a bubble, empty and gay, and shines like a dove's neck, or the image of a rainbow, which hath no substance and whose very imagery and colours are fantastical'. Traherne's childlike and poetic phrases have grown famous in the half-century since he was rediscovered. This lovely mysticism deserves its present reputation:

You never enjoy the world aright, till the sea itself floweth in your veins, till you are clothed with the heavens, and crowned with the stars: and perceive your-self to be the sole heir of the whole world, and more than so, because men are in it who are every one sole heirs as well as you.

Against such translucent sentences as these, there is something a little earthy in the meditations of William Penn, the Quaker, called *Some Fruits of Solitude*, although they contain much practical moral advice and such lovely lines, from time to time, as 'They that love beyond the world cannot be separated by it'.

The Anglican sermon, following unconsciously perhaps the suggestions for simplicity put forward by George Herbert, was restored to a new life with such preachers as Barrow and Tillotson. Barrow, of whom Aubrey has left one of his best portaits—'merry and cheerful and beloved wherever he came' but so absent-minded that 'he would sometimes be going out without his hat on'— is one of the most attractive Churchmen of the later seventeenth century. In preaching he still, however, used the memorable rhythms of the first half of the century; he had not thrown off conscious graces although his message was usually simple and ethical rather than doctrinal. His social advice can be very wise too: 'Jocularity should not be forcibly obtruded, but by a kindly conspiracy (or tacit compact) slip into conversation; consent and complaisance give all the life thereto.' Tillotson, an important figure in the history of Anglican preaching, hardly achieves the height of literature. His solid phrases, clear, persuasive, but oddly ungraceful, mark a turning away from the literary sermon towards the helpful and didactic.

Meanwhile that little secular sermon, the essay, was moving away from the Baconian set-piece or the artfully wrought Character towards the deceptively easy, conversational style of Montaigne. The earliest exponent of the style in English is probably Sir William Cornwallis, whose *Essayes* (1600) were evidently influenced by the

French master. 'My custom is about this time of day to sleep, to avoid which now, I choose to write, so, if this be a drowsie style sleepily done . . .'—the phrase in which he excuses his shortcomings is perfect Montaigne. About twenty years later Owen Felltham, a very young writer who wrote no more in this manner, published his *Resolves*, an unusually charming collection of personal thoughts, easily and gracefully expressed. But it is only with Cowley's *Essays* after the Restoration that the new fashion takes hold of English. His earlier attempts in the genre, a group on Liberty, Solitude, Obscurity, and such subjects, are very stiff, in the manner of Bacon. Then gradually in the essays 'Of Gardens' and 'Of Greatness' his cultured prose breaks down into an artless chatter, and in his essay 'Of Myself' he is as confiding as Montaigne: 'It is a hard and nice subject for a man to write of himself; it grates his own heart to say anything of disparagement, and the reader's ears to hear anything of praise from him.' He did not pursue the style and half a dozen casual pieces are the sum of what he left in this manner. But their influence on Dryden may have been decisive, for Dryden was Cowley's friend, admirer, and junior. It was here, then, that he saw the possibilities of the cultivation of this appearance of the casual.

Dryden's prose, which is scattered through all his works in the form of prefaces to his plays, poems, and translations, shows far less development than his poetry. He seems to have mastered 'the harmony of prose' with such rapid ease that he hardly needed to learn more; the profound considerations in his last 'Preface to the Fables' (1699) are not more perfectly expressed than his earliest reflections on English and French drama in the *Essay of Dramatic Poesy* thirty-four years earlier.

He gave to English prose the note of an easy and well-bred familiarity, and showed by his example that written English could *appear* as spontaneous as spoken, although in reality concealing a consummate artistry in the balancing of sentence, the introduction of metaphor, the breaking and alternating of rhythm. Addison later adapted it to humorous social observation and slight narrative. Dryden used it to argue points of literature and points of morality, a more difficult task. His judgements may be sometimes wrong or sometimes obvious— although he was usually a just and acute critic—but his manner is always enchanting, learned without pedantry, keen without violence, and graceful without affectation. His descriptions of Chaucer and Shakespeare are famous, but even in the preliminary scene-setting which often precedes the serious matter of his essays, there are passages of memorable beauty, like the opening paragraph of the essay on dramatic poesy, in which he describes a journey down the Thames and the distant noise of naval guns breaking the summer silence. His criticism has a surface lightness and a good humour which are particularly attractive. Thus, in condemning French classical drama, he writes:

Their heroes are the most civil people breathing; but their good breeding seldom extends to a word of sense; all their wit is in their ceremony; they want the genius which animates our stage. . . . As the civilest man in the company is commonly the dullest, so these authors, while they are afraid to make you laugh or cry, out of pure good manners make you sleep.

Other essayists of the time were hardly his equals. Sir William Temple, husband of Dorothy Osborne and recipient of her love-letters, expressed sensible views in a cheerful, solid prose which now and again glowed into individual life: 'When all is done, human life is, at the greatest and the best, but like a froward child, that must be play'd with and humour'd a little to keep it quiet till it falls asleep, and then the care is over.' The phrase evidently pleased Goldsmith, who adapted it in his *Good Natur'd Man*.

Much more individual is Halifax, who left in his *Advice to a Daughter*, *Character of a Trimmer*, and *Character of Charles II*, three remarkably fine monuments of what might be called the aristocratic-colloquial manner. Productions of the last twenty years of the century, they are English prose in the manner which Dryden had made possible, but they have an element of conscious restraint, of well-bred understatement that already foretells the ideals of the eighteenth century. He cultivated the compact statement, as, for instance, in his *Character of Charles II*: 'The King did always by his Councils, as he did sometimes by his meals; he sat down out of form with the Queen, but he supped below stairs.' His *Advice to a Daughter* is for its time and period a most wise and affectionate document from a man of the world to a child whom he wishes to see happy in the conditions which inevitably await her. If there is nothing profound in Halifax in a philosophic sense, he has all the virtues and all the sense of a humane and civilized gentleman, and his English exactly conveys his character.

One form of literature lagged conspicuously behind the essay. The novel had gone into a decline about the beginning of the century and showed no sign of recovering until almost the end. It is argued, possibly with truth, that novels and dramas cannot flourish together. Whatever the truth of this, the English novel was submerged by the French fashions which the English drama rode so easily. For twenty interminable years in the earlier part of the century everyone of culture followed the lamentable course of d'Urfé's *Astrée* as volume upon volume came from Paris. When d'Urfé stopped, somewhere about the third decade of the century, Scudéry soon took up the fashion—

> O happy Scudéry, whose facile quill
> Can every year three several volumes fill.

Butler mocked the prolific best-seller, but English novel readers waited obediently for each volume. Incredible that the fanciful Dorothy Osborne enjoyed this dreary stuff; but she did. Far worse was to come. Madeleine de Scudéry was at least efficient and, to those who could penetrate the historical or pastoral disguises which she cast over her characters, as good as a gossip column, for she used prominent members of French society for her models. When Roger Boyle perpetrated *Parthenissa*, the interminable and unterminated work was cheered by no modern allusions. It is not surprising that he was bored with it himself after about eight hundred pages and left it unfinished. His two eastern princes, having each told the other his life-story, are still left standing exactly where they had met at the beginning, neither of them having eaten or sat down during narrations which cannot have lasted less than forty-eight hours. What the real story was going to be, nobody knows.

Sir George Mackenzie's *Aretina* has been saved from oblivion by historians because it contains a curious account of the Covenanting troubles in Scotland ludicrously disguised in Arcadian garb. Congreve entered the field somewhat late in the day with his refreshingly brief *Incognita* which, with its evident parody of the genre, has been held by some critics to foreshadow the more robust mockeries of Fielding.

In the seventies, however, a new kind of novel began to emerge. Its originator, the indefatigable scribbler Mrs. Aphra Behn, has hardly yet received enough credit for the invention, perhaps because she was so evidently out to earn her living rather than to create a new form of art. What she gave to a properly gratified public in *Oroonoko* and others was the long short story or the *nouvelle*. Her aim was to tell a real or apparently real tale in a brief and convincing manner. There is an afternoon's reading in her brisk little books, and the story is in every case natural and convincing, although sometimes a little stifled by a style which has not wholly thrown off Arcadian affectation.

Mrs. Behn had not thought out the *nouvelle* as an art; she did not regulate her pace or her manner to suit her subject; she wrote with a grand, prolific carelessness and no craftsmanship at all. Yet her work holds the reader by its natural vigour and by its astonishing and unconventional realism. There are descriptions as vivid and concrete as any in Defoe. *Oroonoko*, generally considered the best, has other peculiarities; the scene is Surinam, which the author had known as a child and which she described with luxuriant accuracy. Her sentimental comments on the happy state of the native Indians read like an ante-dated passage from Rousseau. Oroonoko, however, is an imported negro slave of royal lineage. He leads a revolt against his white masters for which he is ultimately put to death with gruesome torture. The sympathy of the reader is enlisted throughout for the royal slave; the villains are all among the white men. But for its evident lack of propagandist intention, *Oroonoko* might be an anti-slavery tract.

Mrs. Aphra Behn wrote for and caught the ear of the public that devoured Scudéry and Boyle. But the century's most extraordinary achievement in narrative prose was intended for an un-literary, even illiterate, public. There is no explaining the chance which suddenly produces a writer like John Bunyan, the son of a Bedfordshire tinsmith in a poor village. In a more sophisticated age his genius would not survive the primal corruption of elementary education. In a more barbarous age he might have remained illiterate, and therefore mute, all his life. His only literary training came from sermons, prayers, the Bible, and two books of devotion which his wife showed him, with such old wives' tales as every country child must hear. His natural gift of words he found almost as soon as he was converted, which happened when he was about twenty-five; during the Puritan ascendancy he exercised it in preaching. When he was imprisoned as a dissenter from the Established Church, it was an easy step from preaching to writing. In and out of prison he wrote *Grace Abounding, The Holy War, The Life and Death of Mr. Badman*—the last of which comes astonishingly near to being a novel of contemporary manners—and the extraordinary *Pilgrim's Progress*.

The Pilgrim's Progress immediately touched some universal chord in men's understanding. Its success was phenomenal and not only in England; it was translated into several languages even before the author's death and since then into over a hundred. John Bunyan, pursuing and elaborating the substance of his dreams, had written a universal parable. It was such a thing as only a very simple mind could have achieved so late in time.

The language is sometimes that of the Bible; more often, and more touchingly, that of the simple folk among whom Bunyan lived. There could be nothing more natural than the head-wagging chatter of Christiana's gossips, Mrs. Timorous, Mrs. Bat's Eye, Mrs. Lightmind, Mrs. Know-nothing, and Mrs. Inconsiderate when they seek to dissuade her from going on pilgrimage after her husband. But the language alone cannot be studied with advantage, for there is nothing to be learnt from it. No educated and conscious writer could safely copy Bunyan. His unforced words are the apt instruments of inspired ideas. The symbols which Bunyan chose in his simplicity to convey his meaning have fixed his conceptions as irrevocably as the Biblical parables themselves. It is more than a little absurd to try to place *The Pilgrim's Progress* as literature. It stands outside literature, one of the innocent, inspired creations of man's mind, of which the author and the date seem— and indeed are—insignificant, compared to the message conveyed. The Slough of Despond, Vanity Fair, and the Delectable Mountains have the validity of the great anonymous legends. Yet *The Pilgrim's Progress* combines with this universal allegory the highly personal quality of the novel. Neither Jonson with his humours, nor Defoe with his solid detail, nor the subtlest psychological novelist of this or the last century, has created characters who walk more solidly in our imagination than do Christian and Hopeful, Faithful, Mercy, Christiana, and Mr. Greatheart.

For two reasons *The Pilgrim's Progress* may serve for an ending. First, because it is a great novel, the only

M

great English novel of the seventeenth century. It is in a class by itself, for it has nothing to do with the contemporary novel and was produced independently and in ignorance of it. But it reveals, in its untutored simplicity, how richly suited for the development of the novel was the English language and the natural inventiveness of the English mind. It also shows in striking fashion the way in which native dramatic talent could be turned into a form which is close to drama and yet is not drama.

The English novel from its beginnings until the present day is rich in what are correctly described as 'scenes'; the novel, as the majority of English writers handle it, springs evidently from the same roots as the once fertile English drama, from an interest in the clash of human personalities, from the desire to depict vividly rather than to explore profoundly the actions of mankind in different situations. The dramatic form was shut to Bunyan on account of his religious convictions, but great parts of *The Pilgrim's Progress* are couched in dialogue which is strong enough for any theatre, while the whole conception and treatment is powerfully dramatic. This extraordinary masterpiece demonstrates the close connexion between the novel and the play in English literature. The two forms coalesced in an unforgettable form in the hands of a writer who had never read a novel or been inside a theatre. It may fitly, therefore, close the century and point the way to the age of Richardson, Fielding, and Smollett.

There is another reason for using this great book as a concluding theme. The seventeenth century is the great century of Puritan thought, both in literature and in politics. Puritanism was wholly defeated in politics, in two senses: the Established Church remained established, and the tone of politics and of high society ceased to be religious. But the Puritan outlook with its decent, firm, industrious, practical, and somewhat oppressive code of conduct, its self-righteousness and its corresponding sense of justice and moral courage, had entrenched itself throughout the middle classes. The reaction from Puritanism of which so much is made in descriptions of the reign of Charles II never affected more than a very small section of society. Careful perusal of the private memoirs and letters of the period reveals on the whole a steady improvement in the decencies and proprieties of conduct throughout the century, and the gradual establishment of a diluted Puritan morality through large sections of society, whether Nonconformist or Church of England.

Puritanism is associated—and to some extent rightly associated—with philistinism. The theatre had always led in the attack on extreme Puritanism, and the flaunting in the theatre of a highly anti-Puritan morality induced in the Puritan outlook a certain suspicion of the literature of the metropolis in general. As the years went by, the Puritan-minded perceived that literature had yet another drawback: it was rarely profitable and had no evident usefulness.

But, the English being pre-eminently a literary race, literature continued to be produced in great quantity and quite as much by the Puritan sections of the community as by any other. Indeed, the roots of almost all English literature from the closing years of the seventeenth century to the eve of our own time are deep in Puritanism, since it was the prevailing outlook of that vast middle range of society from the artisan and small shopkeeper to the substantial tradesman, the professional classes, and the lesser gentry among whom the great majority of writers are born.

Puritanism is not in fashion to-day. In the legitimate and recurrent revolt against its philistinism and repression it is easy to forget how much the English literary genius (not to mention the Scottish) owes to this Spartan training. The background of Puritanism created the dynamic, explosive quality of much later English writing. A lumpish, hard provincial Nonconformity opposed itself to the dictates of continental taste and, in doing its fair share of harm, did also much good in preserving native qualities against submergence in foreign fashions, and in creating for the writer the opposition without which he cannot exercise his muscles. The elements of a sublimated Protestantism and Puritanism are the strengthening fibres of the English Romantic movement. They are powerfully present in the nineteenth-century novel and are still with us to-day.

But to return from this diluted Puritanism to the uncompromising beliefs which inspired the seventeenth century: the doctrine of Grace, acting on a constitution robust enough to sustain it, is immeasurably inspiring. It is at once an instrument of discipline and a source of confidence. It has its dreadful side: Milton's character is not sympathetic, and even so simple and human a man as Bunyan surrounds his Delectable Mountains with the whitened bones of the lost. Yet the self-control and the mental discipline which Puritan training imposes, and the intensely uplifting conviction of salvation, are valuable to the writer, the one to control and correct, and the other to stimulate and inspire. An outlook which was, within the same twenty years, the source of two such different masterpieces as *Paradise Lost* and *The Pilgrim's*

Progress is without question among the major forces in the creative art of the world. Its influence on literature in Great Britain has been, and still is, incalculable.

It was the double work of the seventeenth century to perfect and enrich the language and to evolve a singularly clear, powerful, and consistent moral outlook through large sections of society. The country had passed through a political and religious crisis of immense consequence. The violent clash of beliefs and theories was in part at least the outcome of energies too fervid to be repressed. Whatever good or harm was done in this reckless age, whatever else it destroyed, or created, or renewed, it brought forth poetry and prose more glorious, strange and varied than any other time and left to succeeding generations a treasure which cannot be exhausted and which, to this day, has not been fully explored.

BIBLIOGRAPHY

The place of publication is London unless otherwise stated

I. GENERAL WORKS

WARD, A. W., & WALLER, A. R. (Editors). *The Cambridge History of English Literature*, Volumes IV, V, VI, VII, VIII. University Press, Cambridge, 1909–1912.

WILSON, F. P., & DOBREE, BONAMY (Editors). *The Oxford History of English Literature.* When this work is complete Volumes IV, V, and VI will cover the seventeenth century. Of these, only Volume V is at present (1963) available: Douglas Bush, *English Literature in the Earlier Seventeenth Century.* 2nd edn. Oxford University Press, 1962.

Both these works contain comprehensive bibliographies.

CLARK, G. N. *The Seventeenth Century.* 2nd edn. Clarendon Press, Oxford, 1947.

GARNETT, RICHARD. *The Age of Dryden.* Bell, 1932.

GRIERSON, H. J. C. *Cross-currents in English Literature of the Seventeenth Century.* Chatto & Windus, 1929.

KNIGHTS, L. C. *Explorations: Essays in Criticism, mainly on the Literature of the Seventeenth Century.* Chatto & Windus, 1946.

PINTO, V. DE SOLA. *The English Renaissance 1510–1688.* 2nd edn. Cresset Press, 1950.

WILLEY, BASIL. *The Seventeenth Century Background.* Chatto & Windus, 1934.

WILSON, F. P. *Elizabethan and Jacobean.* Clarendon Press, Oxford, 1945.

WILSON, J. H. *Court Wits of the Restoration.* University Press, Princeton, and Oxford University Press, 1948.

II. POETRY

BENNETT, JOAN. *Four Metaphysical Poets: Donne, Herbert, Vaughan, Crashaw.* University Press, Cambridge, 1934.

FREEMAN, ROSEMARY. *English Emblem Books.* Chatto & Windus, 1948.

LEISHMAN, J. B. *The Metaphysical Poets.* Clarendon Press, Oxford, 1934.

MAHOOD, M. M. *Poetry and Humanism.* Cape, 1950.

SAINTSBURY, GEORGE. *A History of English Prosody.* Volume II. Macmillan, 1908.

TILLYARD, E. M. W. *Poetry, Direct and Oblique.* 2nd edn. Chatto & Windus, 1945.

TUVE, ROSEMOND. *Elizabethan and Metaphysical Imagery.* University Press, Chicago, and Cambridge University Press, 1947.

WHITE, HELEN C. *Metaphysical Poets.* Macmillan, New York, 1936.

WILLIAMSON, GEORGE. *The Donne Tradition: a study in English Poetry from Donne to the Death of Cowley.* Oxford University Press, 1930.

III. ANTHOLOGIES OF POETRY

AULT, NORMAN (Editor). *Seventeenth Century Lyrics.* Longmans, 1925.

GARDNER, HELEN (Editor). *The Metaphysical Poets.* Oxford University Press, 1961.

GRIERSON, H. J. C. (Editor). *Metaphysical Lyrics and Poems: Donne to Butler.* Clarendon Press, Oxford, 1931.

GRIERSON, H. J. C., & BULLOUGH, G. (Editors). *The Oxford Book of Seventeenth Century Verse.* Clarendon Press, Oxford, 1934.

MASSINGHAM, H. J. (Editor). *A Treasury of Seventeenth Century Verse.* Macmillan, 1919.

SAINTSBURY, GEORGE (Editor). *Minor Poets of the Caroline Period.* Clarendon Press, Oxford, 1905–21.

IV. PROSE

BUSH, DOUGLAS, & MOORE, C. A. (Editors). *Seventeenth Century Prose, selections.* New York, 1930.

GRIERSON, H. J. C. *The English Bible.* Collins, 1943.

SAINTSBURY, GEORGE. *A History of English Prose Rhythm.* Macmillan, 1912.

SMITH, LOGAN PEARSALL. *A Treasury of English Prose.* Constable, 1919.

V. DRAMA

BOAS, F. S. *An Introduction to Stuart Drama.* Oxford University Press, 1946.

DOBREE, BONAMY. *Restoration Comedy 1660–1720.* Oxford University Press, 1924.

DOBREE, BONAMY. *Restoration Tragedy 1660–1720.* Oxford University Press, 1929.

ELLIS-FERMOR, UNA. *The Jacobean Drama.* 2nd edn. Methuen, 1947.

KNIGHTS, L. C. *Drama and Society in the Age of Jonson.* Chatto & Windus, 1937.

KRUTCH, JOSEPH WOOD. *Comedy and Conscience after the Restoration.* 2nd edn. Columbia University Press, New York, and Oxford University Press, 1949.

NICOLL, ALLARDYCE. *A History of Restoration Drama.* 3rd edn. University Press, Cambridge, 1940.

THE MERMAID SERIES (Ernest Benn) provides useful reading versions of the plays of Congreve, Dekker, Dryden, Farquhar, Jonson, Vanbrugh, Webster and Tourneur, and Wycherley.

VI. SEPARATE WRITERS

Richard Crashaw: *Poems: English, Latin, and Greek.* Edited by L. C. Martin. Oxford, 1927.

Thomas Carew: *Poems, with his Masque 'Coelum Britannicum'.* Edited by Rhodes Dunlap. Oxford, 1949.

John Donne: *Poems.* Edited by Sir H. J. C. Grierson. Oxford, 1912. *Poems, with Letters and Prose Selections.* Edited by John Hayward. Nonesuch Press, 1932.

    HARDY, EVELYN. *Donne.* Constable, 1942.

    SIMPSON, E. M. *A Study of the Prose Works of John Donne.* Oxford, 1948.

John Dryden: WORKS: The poems can be most conveniently read in the Oxford Standard Authors edition of John Sargeaunt (1929); the essays were collected and edited by W. P. Ker, Clarendon Press, Oxford, 1900 ; a selection of the plays is available in the Mermaid Series.

    DOREN, MARK VAN. *Poetry of John Dryden.* Harcourt Brace, New York, 1920.

    ELIOT, T. S. *Homage to Dryden.* Hogarth Press, 1924.

George Herbert: *Works.* Edited by F. E. Hutchinson. Oxford, 1941.

Robert Herrick: *The Poetical Works of Robert Herrick.* Edited by L. C. Martin. Oxford, 1956.

Ben Jonson: COMPLETE PLAYS. Everyman's Library, Dent, 1910.

    HERFORD, C. H., & SIMPSON, P. (Editors). *Works.* Oxford, 1925–51; the first two volumes contain a biographical and critical study: The Man and His Work.

    Five Plays. Oxford (The World's Classics), 1953.

PALMER, JOHN. *Ben Jonson*. Routledge, 1934.
SMITH, G. G. *Ben Jonson*. Macmillan, 1919.

Richard Lovelace: *Poems*. Edited by C. H. Wilkinson. Oxford, 1930.

Andrew Marvell: *Poems and Letters*. Edited by H. M. Margoliouth. Oxford, 2nd edn., 1952.

John Milton: *Poetical Works*. Edited by Helen Darbishire. Oxford, 1952–5.
   English Poems. Introduction by Charles Williams. Oxford (The World's Classics), 1941.
   Selected Prose. Edited by M. W. Wallace. Oxford (The World's Classics), 1925.
   HUTCHINSON, F. E. *Milton and the English Mind*. English Universities Press, 1947.
   LEWIS, C. S. *A Preface to 'Paradise Lost'*. Oxford, 1942.
   MASSON, DAVID. *Life of John Milton*. Cambridge and Macmillan, London, 1859–94. (The standard work.)
   TILLYARD, E. M. W. *Milton*. Chatto & Windus, 1930.
   WILLIAMS, CHARLES. *The English Poetic Mind*, Chapter IV. Oxford, 1932.

Rochester, Earl of (John Wilmot): *Poems*. Edited by V. de Sola Pinto. Routledge (The Muses' Library), 1953.

Thomas Traherne: *Poetical Works*. Edited by Gladys I. Wade. Dobell, 1932.
   Centuries of Meditations. Dobell, 1903.
   WADE, GLADYS I. *Thomas Traherne*. Princeton (and O.U.P.), 1946.

Henry Vaughan: *Works*. Edited by L. C. Martin. Oxford, 1915.

INDEX